GOOD JOBS
AMERICA

GOOD JOBS
AMERICA

Making Work Better
for Everyone

Paul Osterman and
Beth Shulman

Russell Sage Foundation • New York

The Russell Sage Foundation

The Russell Sage Foundation, one of the oldest of America's general purpose foundations, was established in 1907 by Mrs. Margaret Olivia Sage for "the improvement of social and living conditions in the United States." The Foundation seeks to fulfill this mandate by fostering the development and dissemination of knowledge about the country's political, social, and economic problems. While the Foundation endeavors to assure the accuracy and objectivity of each book it publishes, the conclusions and interpretations in Russell Sage Foundation publications are those of the authors and not of the Foundation, its Trustees, or its staff. Publication by Russell Sage, therefore, does not imply Foundation endorsement.

Library of Congress Cataloging-in-Publication Data

Osterman, Paul.
  Good jobs America : making work better for everyone / Paul Osterman and Beth Shulman.
    p. cm.
Includes bibliographical references and index.
  ISBN 978-0-87154-663-0 (pbk. : alk. paper) — ISBN 978-1-61044-756-0 (ebook)
  1. Labor market—United States.   2. Wages—United States.   3. Industrial relations—United States.   4. Working class—United States.   5. Work—United States.   I. Shulman, Beth.   II. Title.
  HD5724.O764 2011
  331.10973—dc23   2011022369

Text design by Genna Patacsil.

RUSSELL SAGE FOUNDATION
112 East 64th Street, New York, New York 10065
10 9 8 7 6 5 4 3 2 1

BETH SHULMAN

This book began when Beth Shulman called to discuss an article I had written on job quality. She was working on similar themes and wanted to share ideas. Over the course of many conversations we found that our thoughts were similar and that are our interactions were enjoyable. We decided to collaborate on a book, but tragically, before we could start writing, Beth fell ill. She died in February 2010.

As all authors know, shape and content change with the writing. This is not the same book that would have emerged had Beth and I written it together. However, the book fully reflects Beth's commitments, and because we spent so much time together brainstorming and planning—some of the most enjoyable and stimulating intellectual companionship of my professional career—Beth is its co-author. I can only hope that the book is one of which she would have been proud and one that reflects her lifelong passion for economic justice.

CONTENTS

ABOUT THE AUTHORS

PAUL OSTERMAN is NTU Professor of Human Resources and Management at the M.I.T. Sloan School of Management as well as a member of the Department of Urban Planning at M.I.T.

BETH SHULMAN was senior fellow at Demos, chair of the Board of the National Employment Law Project, and co-chair of the Fairness Initiative on Low-Wage Work.

ACKNOWLEDGMENTS

This book benefited greatly from the generous support of the Russell Sage Foundation and from their excellent work in bringing it to publication, and I thank Eric Wanner and Suzanne Nichols in particular. Over the course of the research and writing, Elizabeth Chimienti was an invaluable colleague through her contributions to the green jobs chapter (chapter 8), of which she is co-author, and also through numerous stimulating and helpful conversations about the broader themes of the project. Andrew Weaver researched much of the material on community benefit agreements and living wages and did a superb job. Angelica Weiner and Kira Intrator both also provided useful assistance. Hector Cordero-Guzman, formerly of the Ford Foundation, provided excellent advice and support, both for the book and for subsequent efforts to get the message out. Valarie Kniss prepared the charts and contributed in other important ways to the preparation of the manuscript.

I was very fortunate to have the benefit of remarkably thoughtful comments on various drafts from colleagues and friends. For this I thank Suzanne Berger, Annette Bernhardt, Susan Eckstein, Thomas Kochan, Michael Piore, and two referees from the Russell Sage Foundation. The book is much better for this very generous assistance.

CHAPTER 1

Introduction

America is confronting a jobs crisis, and that crisis has two faces. The first face is obvious and greets us every morning when we read the newspapers or talk with our friends and neighbors. There is simply not enough work to go around. Following the financial crisis and Great Recession that began in 2007, unemployment has remained stubbornly high, with devastating consequences. The historian Stephan Thernstrom studied the effect of the Great Depression of the 1930s on the careers of young people who entered the job market at that time and found that they suffered permanent disadvantage.[1] Today's young people confront a similar fate, and their parents, many of whom are out of work, face even more desperate circumstances. The impact on families and communities is incalculable.

The second face of the jobs crisis is more subtle but no less serious. Far too many jobs fall below the standard that most Americans would consider decent work. Nearly one-quarter of working adults–adults, not young people–find themselves in jobs that do not pay enough to support a family at a minimally acceptable level. These people work in factories and hotels, in restaurants and hospitals, on construction sites and in day care centers. The problem spans all races and ethnic groups and includes large numbers of native-born Americans as well as immigrants.

The Great Recession brings home another point: the proliferation of poorly paying jobs affects a far broader swath of Americans than is often understood. Consider the example of Dale Szabo, who in 2011 was fifty-three years old, held an MBA degree, and worked as a manager at Briggs and Stratton.[2] He lost his job in 2003, applied for over one thousand new positions, and finally landed one: as a janitor in the local school district, earning $9 an hour. His comment: "It's very hard work. I never dreamed I would be doing it, but I have to pay the bills." Consider also Monty Blanton, a former electrical worker who, when asked to reflect on the direction of the job market, commented that "the gap between the low and the middle is collapsing."[3]

Mr. Szabo and Mr. Blanton have found themselves in the middle of the low-wage labor market, and their situation is far from unusual. Careful studies of worker displacement show that when people are laid off from previously stable employment, they take a wage hit—if they are lucky enough to find work—of over 20 percent, and this gap persists for decades after the job loss.[4] Americans feel that these risks have grown: successive national surveys show a long-term upward trend in perceived risk of job loss, a trend that remains even after removing the effects of the business cycle and changes in the demographic composition of the workforce.[5] Adding to the evidence is a large literature that examines whether earnings volatility has increased over time—that is, whether people are now at greater risk of sudden falls in their earning capacity. The consensus of these studies is that volatility began to grow in the 1980s and has remained at the new higher level ever since. This is a pattern that prevails in addition to, and separate from, the uncertainty created by business cycles.[6]

The broad relevance of job quality to a wide swath of Americans is also apparent in debates concerning future sources of American employment growth in the face of fierce low-wage overseas competition. Some discussions are focused on emerging industries, such as green technologies or biotechnology. Others focus on programs such as the Manufacturing Extension Service—housed in the U.S. Department of Commerce and replicated by many states—that seek to spur a revival of our manufacturing base. Many of these discussions have centered on technologies and markets, but a core issue is the quality of the jobs they may create. Will these new jobs support families? And if so, what will it take to ensure that this comes to pass? Good answers to these questions require that we understand how firms make decisions regarding the characteristics of the jobs they provide, the public policies that help shape these decisions, and the politics that lie behind those policies. All of these themes are addressed in the chapters that follow.

Job quality is also directly linked to another social ill we confront: widening inequality. When we add up all the nation's income gains accrued from 1979 to the start of the recession in 2007, we see that the bottom fifth of all earners received less than half of 1 percent of that growing pie while the top fifth got over three-quarters. Remarkably, the top 1 percent of earners took home 38 percent of all of the nation's income gain.[7] Inequality in wealth has also taken off.[8]

This remarkable record of growing inequality is due in part to concerns that lie outside this book: the ability of senior management to influence their own pay through manipulation of compensation committees, the capacity of Wall Street to pay itself enormous bonuses, and even the role played by sports and movie stars as they reach for ever more wealth. But without doubt a big part of the story lies in the operation of the everyday job market, and the persistence of low-wage work should be understood in this larger context.

In the years between World War II and the late 1970s, a strong set of institutions helped create and sustain millions of middle-class jobs. These supports have been progressively weakened.[9] Firms used to view their employees as stakeholders whose welfare had a claim almost equal to that of stock owners, but this is no longer true. Unions have been battered and are less effective. The government has steadily withdrawn from its role of strengthening the labor-market floor and upholding employment standards. All of this adds up to a steady erosion of the quality of employment.

The obvious solution is to upgrade the quality of jobs, but our passivity about how jobs are generated gets in the way. Why? To a surprising extent, the obstacles are conceptual and embedded in a worldview that pervades both policy discourse and popular perceptions. One challenge is a belief in the power and correctness of the market. In part, this belief flows from the central tenets of standard economic theory, one version of which is that market outcomes are optimal and the costs of interference are substantial. This presumed optimality has been increasingly challenged, even within the profession, but the subliminal message remains. Linked to this presumption is a widespread belief that policy is doomed to failure. In this view, the lesson from several decades of government efforts—beginning with the War on Poverty and the Great Society of the 1960s and extending to the present time—is that interventions simply do not work. The claim is that even if we wanted to find ways to improve job quality, we simply do not know how. As a result of this thinking, the conventional wisdom that dominates most public debate focuses almost entirely on two strategies: improving education so that people can escape the low-wage job trap, and for those who cannot, providing some level of support through programs such as the Earned Income Tax Credit (EITC), which is an income supplement conditioned on work.

Improvements to education and provision of the EITC are unquestionably worthwhile, but the policy menu they form is strangely truncated because it takes the nature of jobs as given. The basic idea is to let the economy generate jobs of whatever quality is chosen by firms and then, if necessary, to compensate by enabling people to avoid the bad ones or by shoring up people who are stuck in them. But ultimately this approach is naive. There will always be hotel room cleaners and food servers and medical assistants and the myriad of other low-wage jobs. Furthermore, the evidence (reviewed later in the book) is clear that most adults holding these jobs will not escape from them over their working lives. Prescriptions that rely entirely on education and transfer payments will condemn millions of workers to a lifetime of lousy jobs.

We respect alternative perspectives and take them seriously. There is a skills problem that needs to be addressed. There are limits to how far policy can safely push up wages before the costs exceed the benefit. Not all programs work well, and they are often much harder to implement at scale than is suggested by the success of small demonstration efforts. All of this is true. But we believe that it is both possible and desirable to address job quality directly and to encourage employers to provide better work for those at the bottom. There is a great deal of evidence that a combination of carrots and sticks can lead to considerable progress, and we believe that the nation will be much better off for the effort.

How Bad Is Low-Wage Work in America?

How can we define a "good" job? This is a question that many people have thought and written about, and the answers take two tracks. There is a large literature in sociology and economics that asks about the correlates of reported job satisfaction. What traits of a job—wages, autonomy, interesting work, prestige, security, and so on—are correlated with the degree of contentment that people express about their work?[10] This research is interesting, but not really on point for us. We want to know about minimum standards. What is the baseline that we should insist that all jobs provide? There has been a considerable amount of thinking on this second track as well.

Even a casual consideration of this question leads quickly to the conclusion that there is no easy answer and that any measure used is bound to be controversial. What aspects of a job should we consider? What level of each of these characteristics is required? Neither of these questions has clear answers, and the uncertainty is compounded by a series of technical issues, such as how to account for cost-of-living differences throughout the country and for different kinds of families with varying needs. And of course, the question is political since different groups have divergent interests in whether the answer indicates that things are going well or badly.

All this being said, everyone agrees that wages are the most important feature of work, and so we begin there. We use two standards: the poverty line and a measure of relative wages. For the relative wage our measure is the fraction of people whose earnings fall below two-thirds of the median income, and for the poverty line it is the fraction of people whose hourly wage would not get them above the poverty line for a family of four if they worked full-time and year-round.

As we will see momentarily, there is only a modest difference between the poverty line measure and the measure of two-thirds below the median; we have chosen, however, to focus throughout the book on the latter measure (although we present both here for comparison) for two practical reasons. First, as is well known, the poverty line is both conceptually flawed and set at a level well below that needed to sustain a family. Second, the two-thirds-of-median standard is used in many other countries to define low-wage work, and hence using it greatly facilitates international comparisons. Beyond these pragmatic considerations are more principled reasons for going this route.

Figure 1.1   Two Distributions of Hourly Earnings

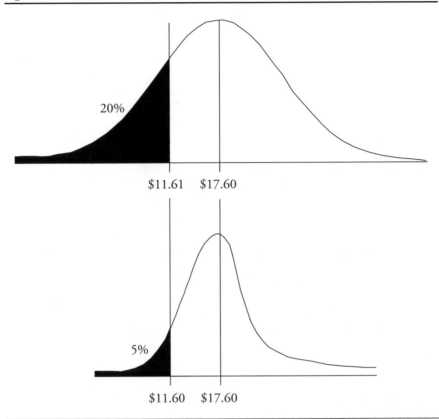

20%

$11.61 $17.60

5%

$11.60 $17.60

Source: Authors' figure.

The core idea is social inclusion: if people's earnings fall too far below the average, then in some important sense they are not part of society. They lack the resources to fully participate, and they are distanced from the ordinary experience of their fellow citizens. It turns out that many Americans share this view about what it takes to be a full participant in society. A recent review of the literature on job quality summarizes public opinion poll data by saying that Americans think the minimum wage is a wage that enables a family to "get by."[11] And in these polls respondents peg "getting by" at a level between 60 percent and 70 percent of the median.

Understanding what it means to fall below the poverty line is straightforward, but the below-two-thirds-of-the-median criterion may be confusing. To clarify the logic, consider the two graphs in figure 1.1, each of which represents possible distributions of earnings. In each graph the median earnings is the same. All that is different is the shape of the distribution below the median. The spread is wide in the top graph: 20 percent of the overall workforce earns less than two-thirds of the median. In the bottom graph a job quality threshold has been set and enforced, and very few people earn below the two-thirds measure. The point here is that the standard we use is about the distribution below the median; our choice of standard has nothing to do with changing the overall median or people's opportunities to get rich.

How many people fall below a reasonable standard for decent work? In this chapter's tables and figures and throughout the book, we limit our calculations to adults between the ages of twenty-five and sixty-four. It is certainly true that there are young people who need to work to support their families, but many others are in casual jobs that are transitory, and it would confuse the analysis to include youth in the analysis. Although we prefer the relative wage standard (falling below two-thirds of the median) for comparison, we also show the results from using the hourly wage that is necessary to lift a family of four above the poverty line. The hourly wage cutoff in 2010 for the relative standard was $11.61 (since the median wage was $17.60), and for the poverty line it was $10.65.

The results of both calculations are broadly similar, as is shown in figure 1.2. The standards translate into 27.8 million adults, ages twenty-four to sixty-four, who earn less than two-thirds of the median and 22 million whose hourly wage puts them below the poverty line for a family of four. By any measure these are very large and very troubling numbers. (The technical details regarding how we worked with the data are provided in the appendix of this chapter. Unless we specifically indicate otherwise, all tables in the book use data from the same source described in the appendix, are limited to adults, and are processed the same way.)

It is also worth noting a remarkable and discouraging fact: in 1983, when the unemployment rate of 9.6 percent was exactly the same as the rate in 2010, the fraction of adults falling below both thresholds was also identical. We have made no progress in nearly thirty years in reducing the size of the low-wage workforce.

Before moving on, it is important to emphasize that we have provided a very conservative estimate of the extent of low-wage work in America. First, our measure does not take into account pensions or health care; as we will see in the appendix, when these are considered, the number of workers in difficulty rises a good deal. Second, many observers believe that it is desirable to construct what they term a "basic needs budget" by starting from the consumption requirements of a family rather than starting, as we do, from the distribution of hourly wages. A recent careful effort to do this concluded that a family of four, with two working adults and two children, would need to have each adult earning $16.10 an hour to meet minimum standards. This is

Figure 1.2   Working Adults Whose Hourly Wages Fall Below the Basic
Standard, 2010

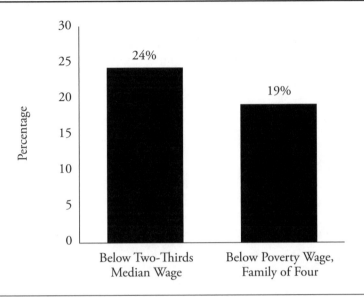

Source: Authors' calculations. See chapter 1 appendix for further details on data sources.

a good deal higher than the wage standard that we employ here. The fact that the number of people in low-wage jobs is so high even using our conservative standard makes the case all the more compelling.

Returning to the standard that we use, who are the people whose earnings put them in the low-wage group, and where do they work? Table 1.1 provides some initial clues using, for simplicity of presentation, just one of the two possible standards.

It is not surprising to learn that women and nonwhites face a higher chance of holding a below-standard job (where "below-standard" means falling below our wage cutoff), since these are the groups that have long faced difficulty in obtaining the best jobs, at least in part because of differential treatment. Despite considerable progress, women's wages continue to lag behind those of men, and occupational segregation is pervasive.[12] With respect to race, there is evidence that even in the low-wage labor market racial discrimination remains a challenge.[13] All of this being said, it is also worth noting that over half of all low-wage workers are white and that 40 percent are men. Although race and gender are clearly important and certainly worthy of careful study, we focus here on the broader structural characteristics of employment that drive the pervasiveness of below-standard work for all groups.

It is also not surprising to learn that better-educated people have better

Table 1.1   *Working Adults Whose Hourly Wages Fall Below a Decent Work Standard, by Various Characteristics, 2010*

	Below Two-Thirds-of-Median Standard	All Workers Below the Standard
All	24.0%	100%
Men	19.7	40.1
Women	28.5	58.1
High school dropout	60.4	21.4
High school degree	35.3	39.2
Some college	22.9	26.9
College degree	8.2	12.4
White	18.4	53.4
African American	33.2	13.9
Hispanic	43.1	28.2
Asian	21.8	4.3

Source: Authors' calculations. See chapter 1 appendix for further details on data sources.
Notes: Whites, Asians, and African Americans are non-Hispanic. Hispanics can be any race. Non-Hispanics who report themselves as multiple races (for example, Asian–African American) are excluded. After these exclusions, the data on race-ethnicity includes 97.6 percent of the population.

jobs. Indeed, the effect of education is dramatic: the chances of holding a substandard job are nearly 60 percent for high school dropouts and under 10 percent for college graduates. In later chapters we discuss strategies for raising people's skill levels, which we certainly believe are important. At the same time, however, we show that if everyone had a college education and nothing else changed, the number of below-standard jobs would not greatly diminish.

We Can Do Better

Throughout this book we return repeatedly to a simple point: that it is possible to redesign "bad" jobs so that they are better. What is normally low-paid work can be improved, and people in those jobs can have a real future. The path from here to there is difficult, with multiple obstacles, both in people's lives and in the environment. But progress is very possible. We saw this vividly when we visited a nursing home that has worked to build a career ladder for certified nursing assistants (CNAs).

CNA jobs are very tough, and the pay is very low. With responsibility for the daily care of patients, a CNA must do a great deal of lifting and carrying, not to mention showing goodwill and patience. The quality of patients' lives depends crucially on the attitude and commitment of CNAs, yet they typically earn about $9 an hour. The CNAs we spoke with were Haitian immigrants. Some had been professionals in Haiti, but others could not do high school math or speak basic English at that level.

The CNAs we interviewed were all in a program sponsored by their employer that would help them move into licensed practical nurse (LPN) jobs, a step that would add about $5 an hour to their pay and give them more varied work. The two-year program involved a day a week of classes the first year and three days a week the second, a schedule for which the nursing home provided paid released time. This program paid all costs (tuition, books, and so on), and many of the classes were taught on-site in order to minimize family and transportation complications. In addition to the formal course work, the employees worked with a career coach who provided a variety of support services. When we visited, twenty-eight CNAs, out of a total of four hundred, had moved into LPN jobs.

The impact of this program on employees' lives was clearly dramatic. We heard comments like, "You can go for your dream," "I have enjoyment here," and "You know you're working in a place that will help [you]." By contrast, some of the CNAs who had worked in other nursing homes said that the employees in those workplaces "came to work angry" because there was "no hope" there. In addition to the training, the CNAs emphasized the importance of the career coach, who taught them how to study and how to manage their time. This person was "someone pushing you to go," someone who "calls you or sends you an email to congratulate you when you accomplish something."

From the perspective of the nursing home, the LPN training program had substantial benefits. People came to work on time and did not call in sick because they were "happy for something." The bottom line was expressed powerfully by one employee, a single mother of two teenagers who had just adopted an orphan from Haiti. She had been at the nursing home for six years, worked in another nursing home on a per diem basis to make ends meet, and had needed to study for and take the GED high school exam in order to qualify for the LPN program. When we asked her how her life would change when she graduated, she replied, "The joy is you've been assigned to a person and one day the person will get out of the hospital because of your care." The lesson from this example is clear: a bad job can be made into a much better one, and there are gains to the employer when this happens. Of course, getting from here to there and assessing the costs and benefits are not straightforward tasks for employers, and we will deal with these complications. But the core lesson is powerful.

Americans Care

In the late summer of 2009, Hyatt Hotels in Boston laid off one hundred housekeepers and replaced them with staff from a temporary help firm. The fired employees were making about $15 an hour plus benefits; the new employees made half that much. The political reaction was immediate. The governor of Massachusetts attacked the hotel and vowed that the state would no longer do business with it, and the city of Cambridge made a similar decision, as did a range of local churches and other organizations. The mayor of Boston described the Hyatt's move as "a crude business decision that will have devastating effects on real people who work hard every day." He vowed that "my administration stands with these workers and will continue to fight for fair wages for all of our people."[14] The *Boston Globe* covered the story intensively, and Hyatt partially retreated by offering the laid-off housekeepers medical benefits for a year.

Hyatt never reinstated the housekeepers, and the reality is that its actions were nothing unusual. As we will see, outsourcing and subcontracting are increasingly common strategies for driving down wages; we return later to the question of what, if anything, should be done about these actions. For now the point is that the reaction against Hyatt's move was broad and immediate. There is also good evidence that popular support for improving job quality and preventing deterioration is widespread, and that this support extends well beyond press statements by politicians and includes the broader public. It is manifested in opinion polls and, more importantly, when people "walk the talk" in voting booths.

The minimum wage is the most visible policy aimed at pushing up job quality, and the polling evidence on it is quite clear: in 2010, in a large representative sample, 67 percent supported increasing the minimum wage from the current $7.25 an hour to $10 an hour.[15] This result is consistent with those of earlier surveys, such as the NBC/*Wall Street Journal* survey in which 64 percent supported a minimum wage increase.[16] In a 2001 survey by Peter Hart, a representative sample was asked how important it was that employers offer a "living wage that provides an income above the poverty line for a full-time worker"—which the minimum wage does not provide—and 87 percent responded affirmatively.[17] Finally, the best evidence of all is how voters actually behave. In 2004, a Florida ballot proposition to raise the state minimum wage was supported by a remarkable 70 percent of the electorate despite the opposition of the governor. Then in 2006, a similar initiative was on the ballots of six states and was approved in every one. In conservative Arizona, 66 percent of the voters approved, while in Middle America Ohio the yes vote was 56 percent. The other states were Colorado, Missouri, Montana, and Nevada. During the same period, legislatures raised the state minimum wage in Illinois and California. It seems impossible to doubt the broad political support for raising job standards.

What Does It Mean to Hold a Low-Wage Job?

Why should we care about the profusion of low-wage jobs? There is an ample literature documenting the health and social welfare consequences of low income, and we will touch on this shortly, but we begin by describing a region of the country where there has been much job growth—of the wrong kind.

If the great cities of Texas would look familiar to most Americans, the same cannot be said of southern Texas and the Rio Grande Valley. For decades, the Valley, anchored at one end by the port city of Brownsville and at the other end by McAllen, was agricultural. The Valley today seems dominated by endless strip malls filled with fast-food restaurants, but the area has benefited from a booming medical establishment, growing government employment (mainly schools), and jobs flowing from trade with Mexico. What has also come to the Valley, in addition to the suppliers to Mexico's factories, are call centers and a somewhat random collection of labor-intensive low-skill manufacturing sites. Job creation in all of these sectors—tourism, health, services, government—is driven by population growth. The annual influx of "Winter Texans"—older people from the North who come to Texas to escape the cold in a cheaper setting than Florida—and the attraction of the beach resort South Padre Island bring tourists to the region. These visitors increase the demand for health care, as does the natural population growth and the influx of new immigrants.

In the past decade, job growth in the Valley has been strong, yet many, if not most, of those jobs have been for very low wages. Between January 2000 and January 2010, employment in the Valley grew by a remarkable 42 percent compared to an anemic national growth of 1 percent.[18] The struggle has been over wages. The median wage for adults in the Valley between 2005 and 2008 was a stunningly low $8.14 an hour (in 2008 dollars), and fully 25 percent earned less than $6.19 an hour.[19] The Dallas Federal Reserve reports that per capita income in the two standard metropolitan statistical areas (SMSAs) in the Valley ranks the lowest and the second-lowest in the nation among all SMSAs (Gilmer, Gurch, and Wang 2001). Among all American counties with populations of half a million people or more, Hidalgo County in 2009 had the highest share of people receiving food stamps, at 29 percent.[20] It is true that the cost of living in the Valley is below the national average, but this cannot obviate the impact of low wages: the cost-of-living difference between the Valley and the national average is between 14 and 20 percent, but wage differences are much greater.[21]

To understand the impact of low wages we visited the area and talked to a wide range of people: four focus groups of residents, three priests, a school principal, and two directors of public health clinics. We came away with a dramatic portrait of the consequences of a low-wage economy.

THE PEOPLE

Everyone we spoke to described the constant struggle to juggle household finances, just trying to get by. One month they might pay the phone bill, and then let that bill go unpaid the next month while they pay the utility bill. Everyone knows how long each company will carry an unpaid bill before cutting services. People spoke of their fear of an unexpected crisis, such as a car needing repairs or an illness. They used the phrase "one paycheck away from homelessness." Even predictable events become crises. In September, with the new school year, people have trouble buying school supplies for their children. Something has to give before they can save the money.

They told stories about themselves or their neighbors. Because they cannot afford day care, their children sometimes move from house to house, between different relatives or neighbors, watching too much TV and sometimes not doing their homework. Older children grow up too fast because they become caretakers for their younger siblings. Couples fight over money. People said, "It breaks the family or it makes the family." Several of the people with whom we spoke suffered from depression and had spent time in hospitals trying to recover. Everyone made comments like, "Every single moment something is on your mind," or "All you think about is which bill is more important."

The Priests

A frequent theme heard by priests in confessions is the strain on marriages because of economic stress. People work too hard, they are stretched, they blame themselves, they blame their spouse. They cannot afford a quinceañera (a party for a daughter turning fifteen). Their children see what other kids have and they do not. In church youth groups, young people question why they should stay in school if all they can get is low-wage work.

The School Principal

Many children are latchkey kids and are unsupervised when doing their homework. Accidents happen, such as when an elementary school student badly burned himself doing a science experiment with only his older brother watching. The father could not take time off from work to visit him in the hospital. Kids come to school sick because there is no one at home to take care of them. Parents miss teacher conferences because they cannot afford to lose the few hours of pay. One student failed to turn in a science project because the parents could not afford the material for a display.

The Health Clinics

The health clinics in the Valley are open to any resident for a very minimal copay. At these clinics, patients can see a nurse or primary care doctor and receive other services, such as wellness training. We talked with the directors about the impact of the low-wage economy from their point of view. The answers were clear. Type 2 diabetes is a scourge in the Valley, and people do not take care of themselves. Because healthy food is more expensive, people eat badly. Even more tragically, because someone with the disease can feel well for many years, people do not spend money on medicine. Then, with the passage of time, they become desperately ill, often losing a limb or their eyesight. In a clinic that has nearly seventy thousand visits a year, the director estimated that half of all patients had medical notations in their record that they suffer from anxiety or depression due to their economic situation. Many times people cannot make it to the clinic either because they are working and cannot afford to lose the time or because the gas is too costly. When they do come, they bring their entire family with them because they have no child care.

A clinic director referred us to an epidemiological study that surveyed Valley residents and conducted blood tests on the sample. The survey respondents were asked about their income levels. The rate of undiagnosed diabetes (that is, diabetes that showed up in the blood test administered by the researchers and about which the respondent was unaware) was three times as high among people whose earnings put them in the lowest quartile compared to people in the third quartile.[22]

Stepping back from these stories, it would be easy to conclude that the Valley is a place of little hope. But this is far from the truth. Teachers stay late to provide a place for kids to do their homework, and they make home visits to conduct parent-teacher conferences. The health clinics work overtime. Many of the people we spoke with have organized, through the community organization Valley Interfaith, to expand training opportunities and conduct living wage campaigns to press at least some employers to pay better. People enter training programs to put themselves in a position to loosen the economic vise. People go to church and build a community. More generally, people speak with genuine hope of a better future. There is no "culture of poverty" and no passive acceptance of their fate. But at the end of the day the corrosive and tragic consequences of a low-wage economy are dramatic and visible.

It would be easy to think that the stories from the Valley are somehow unique because of the region's border location and large immigrant population. But this is not true. A large research literature using national data confirms the lessons. There is an enormous amount of evidence that health outcomes, for both adults and children, are linked to income levels.[23] Indeed, there is good evidence that life expectancy is directly affected by income loss and, strikingly, that the impact extends to the life chances of children of parents in economic stress.[24] This has a direct effect on the individuals affected, but it also reverberates down generations and, for those who care about accounting, ultimately hits the public treasury as people spill into emergency rooms or require subsidized health care. The point is that low wages for some affects us all.

It is too easy to paint the plight of poor people trapped in bad jobs as foreign to the experience of most Americans and not relevant to mainstream debate. But that is far from true. The story of the people in the Rio Grande Valley has a great deal in common with the story we told earlier of Dale Szabo, the former highly educated manager who now works as a janitor.

The costs of low-wage work are greater than the purely material or physical. The political philosopher Michael Sandel wrote: "The republican tradition teaches that severe inequality undermines freedom by corrupting the character of both rich and poor and destroying the commonality necessary to self-government."[25] What does this mean in concrete terms? Consider the example of the father in the Valley who misses parent-teacher conferences and school board meetings because he cannot leave his low-wage, hourly paid job. As such, he is not a full citizen—he does not have the opportunity to participate fully in the life of his community. Ultimately, low wages and high levels of inequality are corrosive to democracy. Certainly the case for raising wages can be made in terms of humanity and basic levels of dignity: in a wealthy nation everyone should be entitled to decent work. But the case is broader than that. We all have a stake in our democracy, and that democracy is at grave risk when inequality explodes and people cannot participate in society.

The Difficulty of Translating These Concerns into Action

Why is it so hard to make progress on improving job quality? One obvious explanation is that it is in the interest of some powerful actors to keep wages low. This is sometimes true, but as we argue later, many low-wage employers themselves feel trapped and under tremendous pressure. For most of them the desire to suppress wages does not flow from greed or heartlessness, but from the real constraints they face. How can these pressures be eased? And what about other obstacles? Politicians and economists who are sympathetic to the need to improve job quality frequently fail to act. Why?

A sense of the challenge can be gained by looking at what happened during the first two years of the Clinton administration. Democrats controlled the White House and both houses of Congress. The minimum wage stood at $4.25 an hour, which at the time was 39 percent of the average private-sector nonsupervisory wage and near an all-time low. (When President Kennedy took office in 1960, the minimum wage had stood at 48 percent of the average wage.) During his campaign Bill Clinton had promised to raise it. Seemingly nothing stood in the way of doing so, and yet, despite pressure from many voices in his constituency as well as from the secretary of labor, the president took no action for nearly two years. What went wrong?

It is tempting to conclude quickly that in the end President Clinton did not care about the fate of low-wage workers. However, this conclusion would be unfair. During these same two years he proposed a progressive welfare reform package (quite different from what eventually was enacted), and he also pushed hard to vastly expand the Earned Income Tax Credit, a program that directed substantial funds to low-wage workers. The real problem, in addition to political pushback from many business associations, lay in the intellectual framework that shaped the debate. The dominant view, among Democrats as well as Republicans, was that it is good economic policy to let the market generate jobs and earnings and then to mop up afterward, if necessary, with transfer payments. In this view, any efforts to change market outcomes should be limited to education and training—that is, to improving the quality of the workforce itself so that people can do better in the unfettered market. This perspective leads to a basic unwillingness to confront directly the challenge of improving job quality. Much of this book is devoted to making a different case. We argue that it is both possible and appropriate to improve job quality more directly and to confront earnings inequality more directly as well.

What History Teaches Us

In making this case, we understand, importantly, that history is on our side. It is not new or unusual to shape or reshape the quality of the work generated by the market. It is true that there is a strong and pervasive popular acceptance of the virtues of the free market, and it is also true that the Horatio Alger myth of the self-made man holds considerable sway. But another equally powerful current in American history points in another direction, toward long-standing and successful efforts to set basic standards, to insist on fairness and equity, and to use politics and policy to improve working lives.

The story of job standards goes back at least as far as the Progressive era. The Triangle Shirtwaist Factory fire of 1911 led to health and safety regulations, and since then the trend has been a steady improvement in employment protections. Employment standards also were put into place, by political means, in the very core of the American economy. Consider the situation at the turn of the twentieth century when workers who sought employment in America's factories faced a daunting situation. Sanford Jacoby, a leading historian, described the so-called drive system:

> The foreman's control over employment began literally at the factory gates. On mornings when the firm was hiring . . . a crowd gathered in front of the factory, and the foreman picked out those workers who appeared suitable or had managed to get near the front. At one Philadelphia factory the foreman tossed apples into the throng; if a man caught an apple he got the job. . . . New foremen might dismiss current employees to make room for their friends and rela-

tives. . . . The foremen relied on ethnic stereotypes to determine who would get a job and which job they would get. . . . Workers often resorted to bribing foremen with whiskey, cigars, or cash. . . . Assignment to a job was determined in large part by favoritism or ethnic prejudice.[26]

By the end of the twentieth century, most employment had been transformed. In both union and non-union settings, strong personnel rules governed hiring, job assignment, and job security. The foreman at the factory gate was a long-forgotten symbol of past abuse. In our terms, "bad" jobs had been made into "good" jobs—not flawless jobs, but nonetheless good jobs. Certainly a large part of this story rests on productivity growth, which created wealth that could in turn flow into higher wages and better working conditions. But productivity had also grown rapidly from the end of the Civil War until the early twentieth century, the time of Jacoby's account.

Part of the story were unions, which pushed many firms to improve working conditions. For example, union contracts often contained provisions governing job assignments, grievance procedures, and job security. These provisions spilled over into the non-unionized sector in part because they came to be perceived as more efficient and in part because adopting them could limit the threat of unionization. It would be a mistake, however, to ignore the role of government in improving the quality of work. Prior to World War II, the Fair Labor Standards Act forced firms to establish uniform record-keeping systems in order to comply with overtime provisions, and the National Labor Relations Board encouraged firms to establish uniform procedures regarding hiring and job assignment to help them avoid being charged with discrimination against union members. However, the biggest government impact came during World War II. The War Manpower Commission required firms to develop staffing plans based on the federal Dictionary of Occupational Titles (DOT), and this led to more orderly job descriptions and promotion paths. The War Labor Board pushed for standardized classifications, permitted wage increases only for merit or equity (which in turn required firms to maintain uniform data and personnel procedures) and encouraged the explosion of nonwage benefits because these were exempt from wage controls.

Even as unions lost influence, the impact of these government policies encouraged uniform personnel procedures that continued to spread throughout the American labor market. In the postwar period the government role in improving job quality grew and expanded into other areas, including the Occupational Health and Safety Act (OSHA) and the Employment Retirement Income Security Act (ERISA). Providing an even more direct example of the impact of public policy on promotion paths and opportunities for career advancement are the equal employment opportunity policies that began with

President Kennedy's executive order 10925 and continued with the passage of the Civil Rights Act of 1964 and many other subsequent pieces of employment legislation. All of these examples should make it clear that the trajectory from a workplace characterized by the drive system of arbitrary supervisory behavior to the workplace that provides decent employment was shaped by many forms of public policy. The government made bad jobs into good ones. There is much to be proud of in this history, but it is a story with several chapters yet to come. The point of revisiting this history here is to emphasize that the next step, improving the quality of work in the low-wage labor market, is of a piece with what America has already done in other parts of the job market. We have a legitimate tradition and much experience in improving work quality, and what remains is to continue the forward movement.

The Plan of the Book

The next several chapters are devoted to developing the intellectual case for directly improving job quality. It is essential to do this for two reasons. First, as already noted, powerful interests and players hold the view that such interventions are inappropriate, and these need to be confronted. In addition, it is important to lay the conceptual foundations for policy and not simply jump into a list of proposals. In chapter 2, we take up what we term the "myth" that has bedeviled action—the myth that market interventions inevitably cost jobs and lead to economic inefficiency. We show that both domestic and international experience give the lie to this argument. We also address three other myths. First, we show that a "rising tide" most assuredly does not lift all boats: even in periods of low unemployment, low-wage jobs held by adults persist in large numbers. Second, we show that when people find themselves in these jobs they have a great deal of difficulty climbing out. Horatio Alger–style upward mobility is a chimera for most people. And finally, we show that the persistence of low-quality work cannot be laid at the door of immigration patterns.

With this underbrush cleared away, we turn in chapter 3 to the argument that the master solution lies in education and training. There is no question that in the long run education contributes to economic growth, and there is also no question that it is good advice to any young person to stay in school. But education and training alone will not transform the low-wage labor market, nor will they enable the adults who are trapped in it to climb out. We carefully review the evidence on these points and show that, if we want to improve job quality, more direct policy is essential.

This logic then leads us to think about the firms that make up the job market, the topic of chapter 4. An easy—and too facile—argument is that firms are greedy, on the one hand, and consistently in violation of employment law, on the other. It is certainly the case that too many firms do squeeze their workforce, and some do violate the law. But the problem is deeper than these concerns. Firms in the low-wage labor market are under intense pressure in low-margin businesses and see only one way of competing: to drive down their labor costs. It is too risky for them to think about another strategy, and in any case they typically lack the managerial capacity to execute it. As a consequence, they use a set of employment strategies that push down employment standards. Of course, there are bad players out there who deliberately violate the law, but the core problem is the low-level trap in which most firms are caught. Policy thus has two challenges: creating an environment in which low-quality work is no longer an acceptable option, and providing firms with the tools they need to operate successfully in that new environment.

What will lead firms to offer better wages and attach jobs to ladders that lead upward? Just posing this question suggests why the answer is so hard. For example, about one-third of low-wage jobs are in small firms, and it is simply not realistic to expect these firms to offer well-developed job ladders. There is a great deal of diversity in the low-wage labor market, and this diversity poses significant challenges for policy. Another source of variation lies in the markets that firms serve. Many firms that offer low-quality jobs are public or semipublic, such as organizations in the large health care sector. These organizations have a real interest in being good corporate citizens, and although this interest is not their only concern—they also worry about minimizing costs—it does offer a handhold for policy. At the other extreme are those firms that are basically invisible to consumers and regulators and with whom the sources of leverage are more limited.

The size and diversity of the American labor market clearly pose significant challenges for policy. It is easy to see why people rail against a one-size-fits-all approach to regulation, and it is just as easy to see why one set of policy prescriptions works in some settings but not in others. It is important to respect these problems, and we do. We describe a policy strategy that has a strong central focus yet is adjustable around the edges for the varying circumstances of employers.

In chapters 5, 6, and 7, we make these ideas concrete. Chapter 5 centers on the role of government: regulation and the deployment of everyday government activities—zoning, purchasing, economic development incentives—in the cause of better-quality work. The next chapter examines the role of voice, unions, and community groups. We then turn in chapter 7 to the question of how to enable firms to respond to these pressures, and we describe a range of training and technical assistance efforts that have shown considerable promise in recent years. These policies can also be tweaked to be responsive to the special circumstances of employers, particularly the large and important small-firm sector.

It is one thing to have good ideas, but as history has shown, making them happen is something else altogether. Progress is difficult and much depends on political will. This raises the question of just what happens when efforts are made to improve the quality of low-wage jobs. What happens on the ground when new jobs are created? What happens when efforts are made to upgrade existing jobs? An excellent laboratory for answering these questions is weatherization work, a traditionally low-paid occupation but one that has grown a great deal, owing to federal support, and attracted the attention of a wide range of advocacy groups that have pushed to upgrade the quality of the jobs. In chapter 8, we report on an in-depth case study of how the struggles to make these new "green" jobs into good jobs has played out in several cities and at the national level.

The final chapter pulls together our arguments and makes a case for the continued importance of creative public policy, which is particularly important in an era when government is under withering attack. We also address a fundamental dilemma: How do we think about a trade-off between job quality and low consumer prices? Is substandard work the price that must be paid to enable consumers to purchase low-cost goods? We acknowledge the dilemma but argue that an open public discussion and political process can lead us as a society toward a solution that respects the importance of decent work.

It is a cliché to say that in a country of America's wealth, widespread poverty is not just unacceptable but unnecessary. But the cliché is true. We are not dealing with the mysteries of curing cancer. If we want to substantially improve the quality of jobs, we have at hand tools that will take us a long way. The challenge is to pick up those tools and put them to work. What we hope to show here is that the problem of low-wage work is large and important, that the arguments put forward against action are fallacious, and that we can make progress if we have the will.

Appendix

In this appendix we first describe the data with which we work and then turn to health care and pensions as additional characteristics of good jobs.

Studying the incidence of job quality requires a large national data set, and the best such source is the Current Population Survey, administered by the Bureau of Labor Statistics, which is executed every month for a very large sample and is the standard source of data used by all researchers and policy analysts to understand trends in earnings and benefits. These surveys collect data on earnings and, in some months, also ask about health insurance and pension coverage. The CPS has some limitations: the surveys do not ask about other dimensions we consider to be important in a good job—for example, support for family care issues—and it is also likely that the surveys underrepresent undocumented workers. Nonetheless, the CPS is the best and most credible source of information available. We use what is termed the outgoing rotation groups (ORGs), in files prepared by the National Bureau of Economic Research (NBER), because these contain the most accurate wage data.

We limit our analysis to people between the ages of twenty-five and sixty-four who are wage and salary employees (that is, not self-employed) and who are in the civilian labor force (not in the armed forces). We eliminate young people because it is well known that many are in transitory low-wage jobs and including them in the calculations would distort our findings. The employment circumstances of the self-employed and people in the armed forces are sufficiently distinct from those of wage and salary workers that mixing these groups would confuse the patterns. There are other technical issues, particular regarding wages, and in dealing with these we follow established standards in the literature.[27]

BEYOND WAGES: HEALTH INSURANCE AND PENSIONS

As we discussed, a job that meets basic quality standards should also bring with it health insurance and pensions. For a variety of reasons, however—some technical and some conceptual—this question is much harder to answer than the question about the wages that people earn.

We can relegate the technical issues to the endnotes, but the conceptual ones are more serious.[28] Consider health insurance. There is a widespread national concern that far too many people lack insurance, and this is certainly justified. According to data in 2007, 15 percent of working people between the ages of twenty-five and sixty-four were not covered by any insurance. (The uninsured figure is larger when unemployed people and children are considered.) Furthermore, many of those who were covered either found themselves paying too much or were covered by programs such as Medicaid instead of through their employer. However, to point out these facts is different from the question we ask here: what fraction of jobs are failing to meet basic standards by providing insurance?

This question is more difficult to answer because data on health insurance are not directly on jobs (as they would be if we surveyed firms) but rather on the decisions made by people who are holding jobs. In the case of wages we can assume that no one is turning down a higher wage that their employer might offer, but this is not true for health insurance. For example, if we observe in our data that someone is in a job from which they are not getting health insurance, it may be that their firm does not offer health insurance, but it may also be that the person turned down such an offer because they are

Appendix Table 1A.1   Employees Without Employer-Paid Health Insurance, 2007

	All Employees	Below Decent Wage Standard	Between Decent Wage Standard and 1.6 Times the Median Wage	Above 1.6 Times the Median Wage
Employees with no employer-paid health insurance	39.1%	67.5%	33.1%	21.9%

Source: Authors' calculations. See chapter 1 appendix text for further details on data sources.

covered by someone else's insurance, such as a spouse. Another example might be a highly paid independent contractor, such as a software programmer. That person would report receiving no health insurance from an employer, but few of us would regard that as a problem. The Current Population Survey data that we must use here (because the CPS is the only nationally representative source of data on wages, pensions, health insurance, and demographic characteristics) does not enable us to make this distinction. The bottom line is that a tally of people who report that they are not covered by health insurance provided by their employer is likely to overstate the problem, yet this is what we must report. There are similar, though less serious, ambiguities with respect to pensions.[29]

Appendix table 1A.1 provides the basic facts. Nearly 40 percent of all employees and a stunning 67 percent of workers below our wage standard do not have health insurance that is at least partially paid by their employer. The last two columns of the table show that the numbers improve as earnings increase, but even among the highest-paid group a substantial number lack employer-provided health insurance (though keep in mind the earlier point about well-paid consultants who are able to purchase their own insurance). It is also worth noting that even after taking into account all forms of health insurance (Medicaid as well as privately purchased insurance) among people below our wage standard, 34.1 percent have no health insurance whatsoever.

When it comes to pensions, the patterns are much the same as with health insurance except that the baseline is much worse: as appendix table 1A.2 shows, 46 percent of all employees are not included in their employer's pension plan. Not surprisingly, the figure is much worse for those below the decent wage standard.

Appendix Table 1A.2   Employees Who Are Not Included in an Employer Pension Plan, 2007

	All Employees	Below Decent Wage Standard	Between Decent Wage Standard and 1.6 Times the Median Wage	Above 1.6 Times the Median Wage
Employees not included in a pension plan	46.8%	77.3%	41.6%	25.7%

Source: Authors' calculations. See chapter 1 appendix text for further details on data sources.

CHAPTER 2

Myths About the Low-Wage Job Market: Clearing the Underbrush

Far too many adult Americans work in low-quality jobs—positions that offer low wages, paltry benefits, and few advancement opportunities. The consequences can be severe for them, for their families, and for their communities. That being said, it is one thing to be concerned about the problem, but another, much harder task to think about the best way to solve it. One challenge is identifying the strategies that can improve economic outcomes for the millions of adults trapped in low-wage employment. Yet another challenge is more intellectual. Many good-hearted Americans would agree that low-wage work is a problem and would want to take steps to address the challenge, but are nonetheless held back because they harbor several misconceptions, or myths, suggesting that the costs of addressing the problem are higher than the benefits. In this chapter, we address directly the incorrect readings of the evidence on which these misconceptions are based and show that they are indeed myths.

Ideas have power, and their sway is apparent when it comes to the job market. Political attacks on active government policy have been growing since the Reagan era, and the handmaidens of this campaign have been conservative intellectuals and think tanks. These players have produced sophisticated policy papers arguing that government policy aimed at narrowing the earnings distribution is unnecessary, either because there is no problem or because leaving markets alone remedies any concerns and active policy has substantial ill effects. These views have been ratified by the seemingly politically neutral mainstream of the economics profession; as a result, a new conventional wisdom has emerged that blocks action. Coherent alternatives to this perspective are few and far between, and the resulting imbalance in debate has left progressives very much on the defensive.

This chapter takes up five myths that stand in the way of serious efforts to address the problem. These are:

1. With high job mobility in America, low-wage jobs are just temporary way stations on the path to a better career.

2. When the economy improves, the problem will be dramatically reduced.

3. The low-wage labor market is driven by immigration, and hence the real answer is to make changes in immigration policy.

4. Policy efforts to alter the distribution of economic rewards inevitably lead to slow growth and damage the efficiency of labor markets.

5. Policy in the American context leads to bad consequences.

None of these myths holds water when confronted with data. This is good news, because recognizing that these ideas are based on misconceptions opens the door to serious consideration of steps to reduce the number of low-wage jobs in our labor market.

Myth 1: High American Mobility Makes Bad Jobs Temporary

The fact that many Americans are employed in low-wage jobs would not be bothersome if there was substantial upward mobility. Such mobility certainly exists in some sectors of the job market. Think, for example, of young people in casual low-wage jobs—movie theater ushers or fast-food servers—who obtain better work as they age. As a nation, we are psychologically committed to this notion of mobility, embodied in the archetypal figure of Horatio Alger, and for this reason many of us do not worry about the size of the low-wage labor market. But Horatio Alger is a myth. The rates of upward mobility in the United States are much lower than most Americans believe, and in fact they are lower than those of other countries.

There is considerable evidence that adults remain confined in low-wage jobs over the course of their working lives. The sidebar describes a series of studies of mobility, and the conclusion is clear: adults in low-wage jobs rarely escape the trap.

When it comes to intergenerational mobility—the relationship between a parent's income and the child's subsequent income as an adult—the United States is much more rigid than most of us would have expected or thought desirable. Of children born in the bottom 20 percent of the income distribution in the late 1960s, 41 percent remained there as adults in the late 1990s.[1] By contrast, the story line is reversed for children born in the top quintile: 6 percent end up in the bottom quintile as adults, and 42 percent remain in the top. This rate of intergenerational mobility is lower than in France, Germany,

Mobility over a Career

One study found that among low-wage earners over six years, starting in the early 1990s (a period of remarkable economic strength), only 27 percent raised their incomes enough to rise consistently above the poverty line for a family of four.[2] A more recent study looked at low-wage earners in the years 1995 to 2001 and found that 6 percent of those working full-time and 18 percent of those working part-time in any year had dropped out of the labor force by the next year. Among those who did stay in the workforce, 40 percent experienced either a decrease or no change in their earnings.[3] Using a third data source, this time tracking mobility from 2001 to 2003, U.S. Department of Health and Human Services researchers found that 44 percent of the employees earning poverty wages in 2001 had no better wages in 2003 and that by then an additional 22 percent were not even employed.[4]

The outcome of welfare reform points to a similar conclusion. Despite the strong economy of the 1990s, former welfare recipients were unable to escape the low-wage labor market. An extensive study of the impact of welfare reform found that "welfare reform—both state welfare waivers in the early 1990s and federal welfare reform in 1996—did not reduce the official U.S. poverty rates of women or children. . . . The big push from welfare to work also doesn't appear to have lifted more people out of deep poverty—defined as living below 50 percent of the U.S. federal poverty line."[5]

Yet another investigation, this time using Social Security earnings data, found that the correlation of year-to-year earnings was 0.9 (close to a perfect correlation of 1.0) and that over a ten-year period the correlation was a still very high 0.7. In other words, people stay in the same place in the earnings distribution, and moving up is rare. The authors concluded that the data "show very clearly that mobility has not mitigated the dramatic increase in annual earnings concentration."[6]

Sweden, Canada, Denmark, Finland, and Norway. Reviewing a wide range of evidence, the mainstream Brookings Institution concludes that "compared to the same peer group, Germany is 1.5 times more mobile than the United States, Canada nearly 2.5 times more mobile, and Denmark 3 times more mobile."[7]

Myth 2: The Problem Will Disappear
When the Economy Improves

In the 1960s, President Kennedy argued that "a rising tide lifts all boats" and used this metaphor to justify ignoring the structural roots of poverty. The basic idea was that the problems of low income and bad jobs could be addressed through policy aimed at full employment. Not only would everyone gain if the economy was strong, but people would be lifted out of the low-wage labor market as better firms, forced by full employment to reach further down in the job queue, hired them and as they gained human capital that improved their productivity. What was attractive about this position was its implication that direct intervention in the operation of markets was unnecessary. Well-designed macroeconomic policy, perhaps aided by investments in education and job training, would do the trick.

Whether in fact this is true is a debate that has never really ended. Even under President Kennedy, and later President Johnson, a band of scholars and policy analysts continued to argue that what they termed "structural" unemployment (unemployment caused by geographic or skill mismatches or discrimination) was impervious to purely macroeconomic measures and that more direct intervention in the labor market was necessary.[8] These "structuralists" lacked political support and were isolated in the economics profession, and in any case the fall in unemployment following the Kennedy tax cuts was seen as vindication of the macroeconomists. The fact that people had jobs but still suffered unacceptably low wages was lost in the debate, and before the issue could resurface the war in Vietnam ended the epoch of social reform that had flourished briefly under Kennedy and Johnson.

But what do we really know? How much of the problem that concerns us in this book can be solved simply by a strong overall economy? When we climb out of the aftermath of the Great Recession, will we put the problems of the low-wage labor market behind us? The experience of the 1990s lets us answer this question with much more certainty than was possible during the debates in the 1960s. As is well understood, the 1990s represented a remarkable period of prosperity. Unemployment steadily dropped, falling from 7.5 percent in 1992 to 4.0 percent in 2000. The 1990s add up to a perfect test of the capacity of a strong overall economy to solve the challenge of low-wage and low-quality employment.

It stands to reason that when labor markets are tight (that is, when demand for workers exceeds the supply of workers), wages will rise and employers will adjust their hiring strategies and standards in order to meet their needs. They can adjust standards because there are very few jobs that require tightly specified credentials or experience (as, for example, in the case of doctors or lawyers who cannot work without a degree or license) and certainly very few such jobs at the bottom of the labor market. Much as we would ex-

Figure 2.1   Wages, Inequality, and Full Employment, Trough to Peak, 1992 to 2000

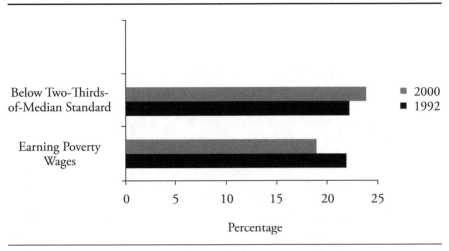

Source: Authors' calculations. See chapter 1 appendix for further details on data sources.

pect, there is evidence that just such an adjustment process occurred in the 1990s. A survey of low-wage employers in several metropolitan areas asked them about the wages, personal characteristics, and skill backgrounds of their most recent hires.[9] The results showed an increase in wages in the 1990s and greater willingness to overlook what in the past had been disqualifying traits, such as welfare recipiency. Some considerations pushed in the other direction as the increased availability of Internet-based testing and background checks led to an increase in screening. Overall, however, the job market for low-wage workers did improve during this period.

But this being said, the question remains: Just how large were the improvements? Is full employment the silver bullet? We just reviewed research showing that upward mobility was limited during the 1990s. More direct evidence is provided in figure 2.1, using the same data that we deployed earlier to sketch the portrait of low-quality work in America.

The figure shows patterns from the beginning to the end of the boom. These eight years of a strong and growing economy led to full employment by anyone's definition. As before, the data are limited to adults between the ages of twenty-five and sixty-four. The percentage of adults earning less than poverty wages (for a family of four) fell very slightly, and the fraction of adults earning below two-thirds of the median wage actually increased a bit. It is hard to look at these figures and think that the low-wage labor market became a much better place as a result of economic growth.

It is important to be clear about the message. Obviously, full employment and a strong economy are important achievements, but they are also limited achievements. Improving the quality of jobs requires more direct policies and interventions.

Myth 3: The Low-Wage Job Market Is Driven by Immigration

The foreign-born proportion of the labor force has surged and today stands at nearly 16 percent. In contrast to the claims of popular discussions, many of these immigrants are very highly educated: 26.7 percent have college degrees, compared to 27.8 percent of the native-born. But it is also true that many immigrants are poorly educated. Among the working-age population, 30.5 percent of immigrants are high school dropouts and a full two-thirds of Mexican immigrants, who account for nearly one-third of all immigrants, have less than a high school education.[10]

These patterns raise two obvious questions: To what extent is the problem of low-wage work mainly an immigrant problem? And to what extent has the surge of immigration pushed down the wages of many natives, hence indirectly exacerbating the problem of low-wage work?

These questions, or variants on them, have excited a great deal of public debate about the place of immigrants in our society, and in particular the issue of undocumented workers. We do not intend to enter into the broader debate about immigration policy, but rather focus here on the narrower question of the impact of immigrants on the low-wage job market. We do, however, want to point out that in no sense is being an undocumented worker a crime in the way that robbery is a crime. Stealing is an illegal transfer that has no social benefit and that no one except the criminal wants. By contrast, regardless of how we add up the pluses and minuses of undocumented immigration, it is essential to remember that these immigrants are here because employers encouraged them to come here—indeed, *invited* them—and that they do essential work for the economy and contribute to the well-being of us all.

Table 2.1 provides data for two years: 1994, which was the first year that foreign-born workers could be identified in the monthly Current Population Survey, and 2010. The data in the table are revealing in several respects. As we saw before, the overall proportion of low-wage employment is quite stable despite the growing importance of foreign-born labor. It is true, however, that the fraction of low-wage jobs held by immigrants increased substantially. This being said, it is notable that even with the growth in immigration, the vast majority of low-wage work is done by native workers. The answer to the first question—is low-wage work simply a problem of foreign-born workers earning low wages?—is clearly no. The answer to the second question—has the surge of immigration pushed natives down into the low-wage sector?— also clearly appears to be no. The probability of a native-born worker holding

Table 2.1   Immigration and the Low-Wage Labor Market, 1994 and 2010

	1994	2010
Overall percentage of low-wage employment	23.6%	24.0%
Percentage of total employment by immigrants	9.8	16.9
Percentage of low-wage work by immigrants	15.8	28.1
Percentage of immigrants in low-wage work	37.8	39.9
Percentage of natives in low-wage work	22.0	20.8

Source: Authors' calculations. See chapter 1 appendix for further details on data sources.

a low-wage job has been essentially stable, even declining a bit, in the face of much increased immigration. A similar exercise, this time using poverty rates, leads to the same conclusion.[11]

None of this is to say that immigration is an irrelevant concern. Immigrants are clearly more likely than natives to be in low-wage jobs, and the fraction of low-wage jobs held by immigrants has grown. But the challenge of low-wage work extends well beyond issues of immigration, and there is no evidence that immigration has made the problem substantially worse. There are several reasons why this would be true. First, immigrants are not perfect substitutes for low-wage American workers; they hold different jobs and have different skills (even if the nominal education levels are the same) and hence have a muted impact on wages. Second, investors are induced by increases in the number of immigrants over the long term to move capital into those areas in order to take advantage of the higher rate of return that follows from a more plentiful workforce and lower wages. Over time, this movement of capital raises the productivity of the employees and hence raises their wages, again muting the impact of immigration on the wages of less-educated natives.

These conclusions are supported by other investigations of the link between wage inequality and immigration. The nonpartisan Congressional Budget Office has examined trends in wage inequality and concludes that immigration patterns did not play a role.[12] David Card, a leading economics scholar of immigration, recently reached the same conclusion that immigrants have had virtually no effect on the wages of natives. According to Card's calculations, because immigrants are concentrated at both the high and low ends of the earnings distribution, they do add to inequality, but in a very small way: the increase in immigration accounted for about 5 percent of the growth in inequality between 1980 and 2000.[13] When it comes to the impact of immigration on the wages of natives with lower levels of education, a recent analysis that takes into account capital movements concludes that only 1.1 percent of the loss of real wages for the lowest-educated native group in the 1990 to 2004 period was due to immigration.[14] Even George Borjas, whose estimates of the costs of immigration are consistently on the high end and who is one of the fiercest critics of immigration, estimates that in the long run, immigrants have reduced the earnings of low-educated American workers by only 4 percent.[15]

The bottom line, then, is that even though immigrants are a growing fraction of the low-wage labor market, they remain a minority and are responsible for neither the stability in the size of that labor market nor the circumstances of natives who work at low wages. There is, however, one complication that does need to be acknowledged: the impact of undocumented workers. This is important because the research just described, both ours and that of others, does not adjust the census and Current Population Survey data to account for what is likely to be an undercount of undocumented workers. Although in principle undocumented workers are included in the sample, common sense suggests that people who, after all, are hiding from authorities are seriously undercounted. The best estimate of the undercount is by the Pew Hispanic Center, according to whose methodology the count of undocumented workers produced by naively taking the CPS data at face value should be increased by 10 to 15 percent.[16] Given that there are about 8 million undocumented immigrants in the labor force, accounting for 30 percent of all immigrants, these are significant numbers.[17] Virtually all of this increase is concentrated in low-wage work, and since the skill levels of low-wage workers differ from those of the immigration population as a whole, some of the statistical estimates of the impact of immigration may be biased.

The Pew study adds weight to a recent survey of employees in low-wage industries in New York, Chicago, and Los Angeles that showed a dramatic concentration of undocumented workers in prototypical low-wage industries: 38.8 percent.[18] These researchers estimate that undocumented workers account for 17 percent of all construction employees in America, 19 percent of all building and grounds workers, and 12 percent of all food preparation and service workers. Within more narrowly defined occupations, the concentrations are even more startling: 40 percent of brick masons, 37 percent of drywall installers, 31 percent of roofers, 28 percent of dishwashers, and 27 percent of maids and housekeepers.[19]

Although it is important to be aware of these complications, it is very unlikely that they overturn the thrust of the main findings. For example, the fraction of natives in low-wage jobs, as shown in table 2.1, remained steady despite the surge in both legal and illegal immigration. Even taking the undercount into account, undocumented workers are only 5.4 percent of the total civilian labor force; moreover, they are likely to be even worse substitutes for native workers than are legal immigrants. Hence, while undocumented workers are an important element in the low-wage labor market, they are not the main story, and their impact on the earnings of natives is modest.

Myth 4: Policies to Improve Job Quality Hurt Economic Performance

One critique of any effort to improve job quality and reduce the size of the low-wage labor market is that such actions distort incentives and damage overall economic performance. This line of thinking is based on the idea that people work harder and invest more if they fear the consequences of not doing so. The threat of low wages provides the incentives that will prod people to produce more. Certainly in the past decades much conservative thought has bought into this view, which has also underwritten the critique of social policy. There is, however, an argument on the other side: people respond better to the carrot than to the stick, and if working conditions are improved, effort and productivity will rise. We return to this point later in the book, but here we ask whether the evidence supports the double-edged critique that inequality improves overall job market performance and that policies that reduce inequality make matters worse.

A good way to test these arguments is to examine the performance of several northern European nations, all of which have achieved the same level of technological sophistication as America and all of which compete in international markets. The United Kingdom, France, and Germany are the largest continental economies, and the United Kingdom is most similar to the United States in terms of its lack of commitment to policies aimed at raising the floor of the job market. Denmark, the Netherlands, and Sweden are all considerably smaller, but they are open economies exposed to the forces of international competition. How does America compare to these nations in terms of the incidence of below-standard work? Figure 2.2 shows the ratio of the earnings of the top 10 percent of wage earners to the bottom 10 percent, as well as the ratio of the median to the top 10 percent. It is clear that the United States is the outlier with respect to the gap between the bottom and the top, and even between the top and the middle. Given these patterns, it is not surprising that the poverty rate in the United States substantially exceeds that of other developed nations.[20]

Why does the United States have a larger fraction of jobs paying low wages than other nations? One answer might be that on average the skill level of European employees is higher than the average skill level of U.S. workers, perhaps owing to immigration or other factors, and that wage patterns reflect this. However, a recent study using international comparisons of literacy and education levels showed that such skill gaps account for virtually none of the difference in earnings patterns.[21] Other commonly cited differences between the United States and Europe are not directly relevant. It is true that most European nations have larger transfer systems than we do—that is, their welfare states are more extensive—and that they provide more in the way of child care, parental leave, and the like. But the gap of interest to us here is the

Figure 2.2   Earnings Dispersion, 2007

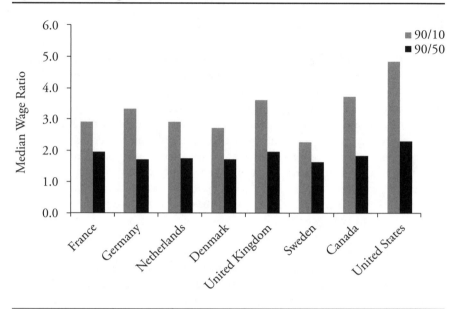

Source: Authors' calculations based on data from *OECD Employment Outlook* 2009 (OECD, various years).

gap in job pay rates, and these are only indirectly affected by the varying patterns of the welfare state. What is really at play here is that the European nations tend more directly to influence the wages and working conditions at the bottom of the job market than the United States does. The key differences are the scope of collective bargaining, the level and reach of the minimum wage, and regulations regarding the quality of temporary and part-time work.[22]

Do Europeans pay a price for pushing up the bottom of the job market? The best measure of the success of an economy in generating jobs for its citizens is the employment-to-population ratio—the fraction of the population that works. Figures 2.3 to 2.6 show the trajectory of this measure from the mid-1990s through the late 2000s for so-called prime-age workers between twenty-five and fifty-four. The advantage of focusing on prime-age workers is that it eliminates school-age youths, since the educational systems of these countries differ greatly in terms of how the working patterns of youth are formally organized while they are in school. For ease of reading, and also to make the point even clearer, the figures are presented in pairs, for both men and women: one figure compares the United States with the larger European economies and the other compares the United States with the smaller ones. The conclusions hold in every case.

It is apparent that there is no basis for claiming that the much larger U.S.

Figure 2.3   Employment to Population, Men Ages Twenty-Five to Fifty-Four, 1995 to 2009

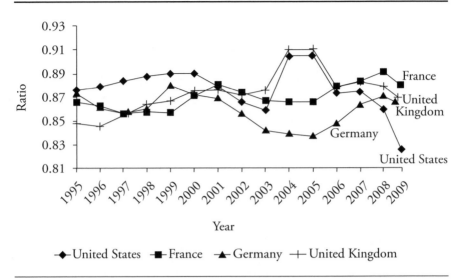

Source: Authors' compilation based on data from *OECD Employment Outlook* (various years).

Figure 2.4   Employment to Population, Men Ages Twenty-Five to Fifty-Four, 1995 to 2009

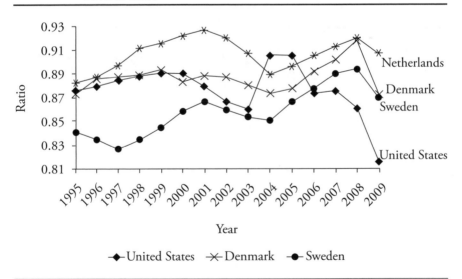

Source: Authors' compilation based on data from *OECD Employment Outlook* (various years).

Figure 2.5   Employment to Population Ratio, Women Ages Twenty-Five to Fifty-Four, 1995 to 2009

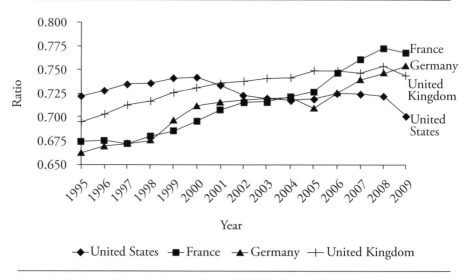

Source: Authors' compilation based on data from *OECD Employment Outlook* (various years).

Figure 2.6   Employment to Population Ratio, Women Ages Twenty-Five to Fifty-Four, 1995 to 2009

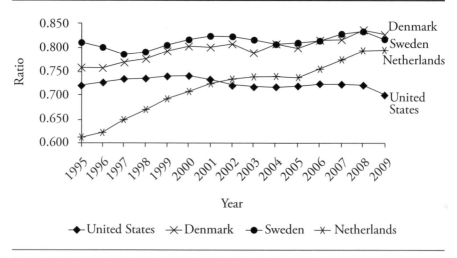

Source: Authors' compilation based on data from *OECD Employment Outlook* (various years).

low-wage labor market enables us to deliver more jobs to our citizens; if anything, we typically do worse. Other researchers looking at different measures reach similar conclusions. As the Harvard labor economist Richard Freeman wrote, "The best summary of the data—what we really know—is that labor institutions reduce earnings inequality but that they have no clear relation to other aggregate outcomes, such as unemployment."[23]

Myth 5: Policy in the American Context Leads to Bad Consequences

The foregoing discussion used international comparisons to show that economies with greater levels of fairness do not suffer adverse consequences with respect to labor market performance. But what happens when we look more carefully at just the U.S. experience? Do interventions to improve job quality damage the functioning of our job market? A good way to think about this is to briefly review the evidence on the minimum wage, which is, after all, the longest-standing and most direct policy aimed at improving job quality in the bottom of the labor market. We will see that attacks on the minimum wage miss the mark; in fact, increases in that standard do not have the negative effects attributed to it by critics.

The conventional way of thinking about the benefits of the minimum wage is that it not only increases earnings for those whose prior wage was below the minimum but may also, for a couple of reasons, ratchet up wages above the minimum if it leads employers to adjust other earnings upward. First, within many firms there is a wage structure—that is, there is a relationship between wages for different occupations and hierarchical levels. If wages for one job or level are pushed up, then the firm maintains the relationships by raising the other wages. This makes economic sense if worker effort and commitment and the ability to recruit and retain is influenced by relative wages, and there is a great deal of evidence that this is true. The other reason wages may rise for those already earning above the minimum is a bit more abstract but no less real. In a large and complex labor market it is hard to know what the "right" wage is, and employers often look for something on which to anchor this determination. The minimum wage may serve that function, and when it rises, the overall wage structure, at least for the jobs in the region of the minimum, shifts up.

The cost side is straightforward. Standard economic theory is clear that when wages are forced up above their free market rate, jobs are lost as firms lay off—or no longer hire—employees whose productivity falls below the newly required pay. This may also happen because employers are less willing to spend resources on training aimed at improving productivity because they are being forced to spend more on direct compensation. There may be an additional negative effect as prices are forced up: the consequent reduction in demand may lead to reductions in employment.[24] It is typically thought that the negative effect falls most heavily on young people because they work in low-wage sectors and also because they are inherently less productive and more in need of training.

Framed in these terms, the debate seems to become purely empirical, just a matter of adding up the costs and benefits. However, it has not been so simple. Sometimes the strength of prior beliefs about the negative consequences of the minimum wage has been so strong that a great deal of writing, in textbooks as well as in policy documents, has taken the form of assertions from theory rather than from research. More importantly, measuring these impacts is complex, and different methodologies produce somewhat differing assessments. Until relatively recently, the consensus among economists was mixed: increases in the minimum wage lead to modest job loss, they agreed, particularly among teenagers, but low-wage workers as a group benefited because the sum of the higher wages was larger than the aggregate costs of the job loss.[25] This mixed verdict left the question open, and advocates on both sides continued to engage in the same debates.

In the last decade, the weight of the evidence has shifted in the direction of supporters of a strong binding minimum wage. This shift was driven by two important bodies of empirical work, research emanating from the heart of the labor economics profession.

The first important set of findings came from efforts to understand why wage inequality exploded in the 1980s, a period when the relative wages of those at the bottom of the wage distribution sharply fell. Although the initial instinct of researchers was to focus entirely on the pattern of the demand for education and skill, a consensus has emerged that the declining value of the minimum wage was an important part of this story. The initial work along these lines found that, for the 1980s, the decline in the real value of the minimum wage explained one-quarter of the growth in wage inequality for men and nearly one-third for women.[26] More recent estimates somewhat reduce the estimated impact for men and increase it for women.[27] The implication of these findings is clear: if the goal is to reduce inequality, then the fall in the value of the minimum wage was a bad thing and an increase would be good. Put more directly, people at the bottom of the job market clearly benefit from a strong minimum wage.

Confirmatory evidence is provided by several important recent studies. David Card and Alan Krueger examined the employment impact of the minimum wage in a clever set of experiments in which they compared employment outcomes in fast-food restaurants that were located close to each other, and hence in the same markets, but were in different states, one of which had just raised its minimum wage. In addition, they used national data across states to examine the impact of varying state minimum wage levels on employment outcomes.[28] Their findings with respect to employment levels overturned conventional wisdom: the impact was basically zero, and in at least some cases the impact was even positive. More recently, Arindrajit Dube, T. William Lester, and Michael Reich examined employment patterns in all contiguous counties in the United States that varied in their level of minimum wages and found no negative employment impact.[29]

There are several reasons why the minimum wage might not have the effect broadly predicted by economic theory. One is that when firms engage in wage-setting they have more margin to increase or lower wages than theory predicts. This idea of a "zone of indeterminacy" was put forward and documented by an earlier generation of labor economists. Firms enjoy a range of discretion in setting their wages, with some choosing, for a variety of reasons, to pay at the high end while others choose to pay at the low end. What are those reasons? Higher wages guarantee a queue of job applicants for openings so that costly vacancies are minimized. Higher wages lead to less turnover and greater commitment and effort. Higher wages improve a firm's reputation in the community. For some firms these reasons are compelling. What a higher minimum wage does in effect is to push lower-paying firms into what might be termed a "high pay equilibrium."

This formulation points to a second reason why the minimum wage does not have the pernicious effects predicted. Again drawing on the ideas of the earlier generation of economists, there is evidence that when firms are forced to increase their pay they respond by improving their practices and hence their productivity in order to compensate. This "shock effect" ameliorates the impact of the minimum wage. Of course, for this idea to make sense it must be the case that firms are not operating as efficiently as possible and that there is room for improvement beyond the standard channel of capital deepening, which would lead to job loss. The notion that there is room for operational improvement is standard fare in business schools and the management consulting world, and there is broad evidence that it is true. These points will also be important when we turn in later chapters to a discussion of policies aimed at encouraging, and compelling, firms to upgrade their employment practices.[30]

There is a deeper argument regarding the minimum wage and other labor market standards. Standards set norms: they establish broad expectations about what is right and acceptable behavior. These norms are not always obeyed—no norms always are, whether they are about jobs or child-rearing or behavior in a sports contest—but they are important and have an influence that should not be underestimated. Moreover, labor market standards help set norms. Research using national data on minimum wage increases shows that minimum wage norms are important,[31] and the experience of communities that have passed local minimum wage or living wage laws also supports this conclusion.[32]

The bottom line is that the minimum wage can be an important instrument for improving the economic circumstances of employees in the low-wage job market. Does this mean that there are no limits to how high we can safely increase the minimum wage? Of course not. It is obvious that there is some limit, that (to be extreme) a minimum wage of $25 an hour would be damaging. But what is this limit? There is no certainty about this, but what we do know is that we are not there yet and in all likelihood are well below it.

Conclusion

The myths that block action to address the low-wage job market are just that—myths. Mobility out of low-wage work is low. Immigration is not the cause of the problem. Full employment will not solve it either. And policies that do seek to reduce the incidence of bad jobs do not inevitably lead to economic underperformance. The American experience with the minimum wage shows that it does not lead to job loss.

All this being said, it is certainly true that poorly conceived labor market regulation can be deleterious. As an example, laws that prohibit employers from laying off employees when there has been a substantial downturn in the market can have the unintended effect of providing strong disincentives against hiring new workers when they are needed. A more constructive policy would be a generous and well-designed unemployment insurance program combined with assistance in finding new work and obtaining any needed new skills. But to say that some regulations and standards can be bad does not imply that all regulations and standards are to be discarded. In fact, there is good evidence that well-designed policy can have positive impacts.

There are a range of reasons why well-designed standards and regulations can be good policy. Sophisticated economic theory understands that employers often have power in the labor market—that is, they have discretion over compensation levels and also can collect excess profits, owing to their power in product markets. Most firms would like to keep the surplus for their shareholders, but this of course raises a question of distributional fairness. Well-designed standards and regulations can help ensure that employees obtain a reasonable share of these profits.

There is also good reason to believe that well-designed standards can actually improve economic performance. Employees who are healthy, who are safe from occupational injuries, and who believe that they are treated fairly work harder, are more committed to the firm, and have lower turnover rates and higher productivity. There is good evidence on all of these points, which we discuss later in the book, but first, in the next chapter, we take up another common misconception: investing in education and training is an adequate response to the challenge of low-wage work. We show that, while skill is important, it is far from a magic bullet and that changes in employers' employment practices are essential.

CHAPTER 3

Do You Get What You Deserve? The Role of Education and Skill

Why are so many jobs of low quality? Why do so many people find themselves trapped in these jobs? Much of the literature and a great many commentators believe that the answer lies in the education and skills of workers themselves. In his 2010 State of the Union address, President Obama said, "The best antipoverty program is a world-class education," and in making this assertion the president neatly captured what is certainly the dominant strain of thinking about the challenge of low-wage work.

Scholars and policymakers point to the correlation between education and wages and argue that, if people had more human capital, they would not find themselves in bad jobs. Closely related to this view is the argument that the trajectory of technological change has hollowed out the middle, increasing the demand for workers with high-level skills and, perhaps paradoxically, also increasing the demand for low-skill jobs that by their very nature can only command low pay. Thus, in this view, the problem is a combination of inevitable market forces and the skill deficits of workers. The solution lies in education and training, not in any shifts in how markets are governed or in how firms do business.

There is, however, an alternative perspective, one that points to a different set of considerations. Education and skill are unquestionably important, as we will see, but the pure human capital story is incomplete because it can explain only a limited fraction of the variation in labor market outcomes. To obtain a fuller understanding of what generates and maintains low-quality work, we need to examine how firms make decisions about organizing work and providing jobs of a certain quality. Penetrating the decision-making calculus of firms is crucial for developing a more complete and sophisticated view of the factors that drive job quality and the constructive steps forward that are possible.

In this chapter, we discuss the education-skill argument. Then, in chapter

4, we look at how firms go about organizing work and how their choices affect the quality of jobs.

Skill

Echoing the remarks cited earlier of President Obama, former Federal Reserve chairman Alan Greenspan told the standard story when he said that inequality is "a problem caused basically by our skill mix not keeping up with the technology that our capital stock requires."[1] Even a progressive foundation argued in a report that, "without the proper skills, training and education, many American workers cannot share this nation's prosperity."[2] In this view, people earn low wages because their skills do not justify better pay. For both individuals and for society, the solution is to increase individuals' skills through schooling and, for those past school age, through training. If we add to this recipe other aspects of individuals' human capital—for example, their attitudes and work ethic—then we have the package of personal improvements that will solve the problem.

Virtually all public policy aimed at addressing the problem of low wages has this supply-side flavor: improve the skills of the workforce. There is a distasteful strain of blaming the victim in this line of thinking—people earn lousy wages because they do not deserve any better—but if we can get past this particular spin or tone, we see that there is certainly considerable validity to the claim. There is no question that the educational attainment of Americans has gone up over the decades, and this improvement reflects the fact that our economy is demanding more and better skills from its workforce. In 1950, 9.2 percent of the labor force had some college education and 7.8 percent had a college degree, yet by 2000 these figures stood at 32 percent and 29.7 percent, respectively.[3] Even casual reflection reveals that many jobs are more complex today than they were in 1950 and that, on average, skill demands have grown. An extensive scholarly literature confirms this observation.[4]

Better education, improved skills, and, at least in some cases, improved behaviors are part of the solution. It is common sense to believe that there is a link between a worker's productivity and what he or she can command from the job market, and it is also common sense to believe that education is linked to productivity. The most basic evidence supporting these beliefs is the simple relationship between education and wage levels. Figure 3.1 shows the average hourly wage in 2010 for employees with different levels of education.

An extensive (to put it mildly) literature addresses the possibility that educational attainment is simply a proxy for preexisting skills or abilities, and the relationship between education and earnings remains strong. Additional support for the need for improved skills comes from conversations with employ-

Figure 3.1   Median Hourly Wages for Different Education Levels, 2010

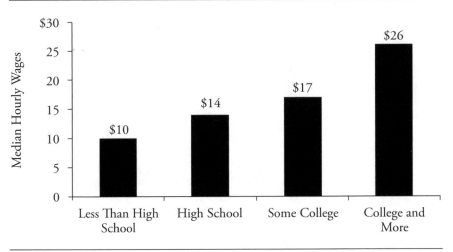

Source: Authors' calculations. See chapter 1 appendix for further details on data sources.

ers as well as with advocates for the working poor who manage programs aimed at helping them move up job ladders in their organizations. Chapter 7 directly takes up the question of what is required to construct these career ladders, and training is a prominent part of the discussion.

All this being said, we need space for another perspective. Skills, though a part of the story, are far from being the entire explanation, nor do skills provide an adequate intellectual basis for a policy strategy. Indeed, the role of education in explaining the persistence of low-wage work is often exaggerated. There is ample scope to consider additional strategies for improving wages and benefits beyond a single-minded focus on the characteristics of employees. Policies aimed at shifting the nature of labor demand deserve to be featured in any discussion. To see this, we need to understand the limits of the skill-education story, which, because it is so commonly accepted in both the policy and the academic worlds, distracts attention away from other important ways of thinking about the problem and its solutions.

Beyond Education and Behavior

Education and skill are obviously significant, but the story does not end there. One clue that the story is incomplete comes when we probe more carefully the relationship between education and earnings. It is clear from figure 3.1 that on average there is a relationship between education and earnings,

Figure 3.2   Hourly Wage Distribution for Men and Women Ages Thirty-One
to Thirty-Nine, High School Degree Only, 2010

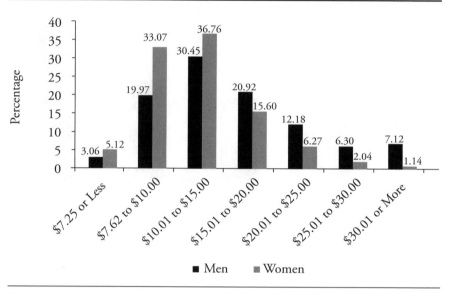

Source: Authors' calculations. See chapter 1 appendix for further details on data sources.

but this average masks a great deal of variation. To illustrate this point, figure
3.2 shows the distribution of earnings among thirty-one- to thirty-nine-year-
old men and women with only a high school degree. As the figure makes
clear, even within these very narrowly defined groups there is a great deal of
variation in earnings, and this variation cannot be explained by education,
age, or gender since these are controlled for in the figure. More sophisticated
statistical analyses reach the same conclusion.[5]

One response to these complications is to argue that human capital is a
multidimensional construct and that education is an incomplete measure of
the full range of human capabilities rewarded in the job market. Personality
and behavior also matter, and it is not hard to come up with a list of important traits, such as diligence, ability to cooperate with supervisors and fellow
workers, and self-confidence. The literature that studies the relationship between these characteristics and earnings is less extensive than the focus on
years of education, but nonetheless the evidence seems clear that certain traits
do exert an independent impact on labor market success. In fact, a recent review of this literature found that personality and behavioral variables were
frequently more important than measures of education or cognitive ability in
explaining earnings, a finding that is problematic for standard human capital

stories.[6] Employers often make the same point, and many interviewed for this book expressed real concerns about the difficulty of finding employees with the proper behaviors. In national surveys, employers confirm this impression by ranking attitudes higher than educational attainment.[7]

Nonetheless, as was true for the simple years-of-schooling measure, the question remains: How important are these traits in explaining overall wage patterns? Would controlling for all of these other personal characteristics compress the wage distribution shown in the chart? Such a compression would mean that the (augmented) human capital story does indeed explain most of the variation across people in wages. There are not very many sources of data that provide extensive measures of personality, but one of the few is the Panel Survey on Income Dynamics (PSID), a nationally representative survey that followed thousands of people over many years. In an analysis of these data, researchers looked at the impact of both education and a substantial array of personality measures on earnings.[8] In addition, the statistical model included variables measuring the respondents' health status and family background. When all of these variables were entered into a model estimating wages, only one-third of the variance in wages was explained. Another study using two different data sets, each of which included a range of personality variables, was able to explain only about one-quarter of the variance in wages.[9]

Additional evidence that more is at play than personal characteristics comes from a series of investigations that estimated models of wage determination by combining data on individuals with data on the firms in which they worked. These researchers consistently found that a very substantial fraction of wage variation is due to firm characteristics and not to the human capital of the employees.[10] Related to this pattern—and providing additional support for the argument that more than human capital is at work—are studies that show that firms have what might be termed a wage policy: if one occupation is paid above (or below) the average market wage for that job, then all occupations in the firm enjoy the same premium (or suffer the same reduction).[11] Such wage policies cannot be explained in human capital terms, since both market conditions and skill requirements vary across the different occupations.

Education and Training Cannot Eliminate Low-Skill Work

The foregoing suggests that the persistence of a low-wage labor market, and the wide distribution of earnings that this implies, cannot be easily explained by a single-minded focus on human capital. Another way of making this point is to ask what would happen if somehow we were to radically increase the number of people with a college education. Would this eliminate the low-skill/low-wage labor market problem? The rub here is that all of the evidence commonly cited about the benefits of education focuses on what economists call the margin, that is, what might happen if one additional individual improved his or her education. Telling your nephew to stay in school is clearly good advice. But perform a thought-experiment: If all the employees in low-wage jobs suddenly acquired a community college degree or better, would the jobs they hold disappear? Would all of their wages rise? The exact answer to this question differs depending on the time horizon, but over any reasonable period the answer would seem to be no.

For the short or medium run, one way to think about the question is to consider what would happen to, say, the job of chopping lettuce in hotel kitchens. Would this work suddenly become "good"? Would wages go up? One source of wage increase might be the greater efficiency of these suddenly better-educated employees, who might do a better job of planning their work patterns. But the gains from this source seem very modest, if they even exist. Another source of gain might be the decision of employers to take advantage of a more-educated workforce by installing better capital equipment, hence increasing productivity, but here too the possibilities seem modest at best. Furthermore, given the limit on how much customers are willing to pay for salads, the margins for substantial pay increases seem small. In short, over the working lives of many lettuce-chopping employees, it is hard to see much gain in kitchen jobs when education levels rise.

In the very long run, the general increase in education might encourage employers in other sectors of the economy to invest in technologies that make use of new skills, and this could create openings that lead employees to leave kitchen work and move to the better opportunities. This is the broad idea behind the belief that education leads to economic growth, and there is a theoretical basis for believing that such an outcome is possible.[12] However, this trajectory is of little help to adults working today in low-wage jobs, and perhaps not even to their children.

Moving from thought-experiments to believable numbers is very difficult because standard economic survey data on individuals are of little use in answering questions about nonmarginal shifts and the path of economy-wide growth and change. The best hard evidence is the literature on education and economic development. We think that, in the long run, a society grows richer as it increases its education level, although even here the evidence, as one recent review noted, is surprisingly "fragile."[13] The same review concluded that the link is probably valid but also that the process takes a long time. Drawing on this literature, a recent simulation found that if the United States could increase its ranking on standardized literacy test scores over a twenty-year period, from the middle of the OCED pack to the top, then over the same period our GNP would increase by 5 percent from what it would otherwise be.[14] This would be an important achievement and over a longer time span would compound into a considerable gain. But from the perspective of improving conditions in the low-wage labor market over a period that would affect today's generation of workers, the impact is modest.

The Trajectory of Skill: Will There Be Opportunities for Low-Wage Workers?

Will there be good jobs to which low-wage workers can aspire, or is the trajectory of technological change creating a situation in which the only jobs available will be either very low-skill or very high-skill, with few opportunities in the middle? In taking a look at this important question, a recent line of research has claimed that the latter situation, dubbed "polarization," characterizes our future. We believe that this is incorrect.

The polarization story emerged as an explanation for the apparent failure of earlier models linking education to inequality. These models worked well in explaining the patterns in the 1980s, but beginning in the 1990s, significant problems emerged. People with a high school degree or less held their own relative to the median wage, a reversal of the pattern in the 1980s, when the bottom fell out of the high school labor market. In addition, and very problematic for the education story, is that the wages of those with just a college degree (as opposed to an advanced degree) have stagnated. In the surveys between 2000 and 2009 with which we have been working, the hourly wage of those with a college degree increased by a total of 0.3 percent, while the hourly wage of those with only a high school degree grew by 1.9 percent and the wage of those with a graduate degree by 2.7 percent.

The explanation that emerged was grounded in ideas about the impact of computer technologies.[15] The argument was that computers eliminate routine work that can be adequately captured by algorithms and that these tend to be middle-skill jobs (such as clerical work or assembly-line work). What is left is a growing demand for service work at the bottom (for example, washing floors or caring for the elderly) that cannot be computerized and highly skilled work at the top (senior managers or investment bankers). Hence, jobs are growing at the bottom and the top of the skill distribution, wages at the bottom are holding their own relative to the middle, and wages at the top have pulled away from the middle.

There is certainly some truth to this story, and it is a creative idea. In particular, service-sector jobs are growing as a proportion of the economy, although it should also be noted that this does not prove the argument about computers. The demand for service occupations can grow for numerous reasons, such as the aging of the population and the changing demand for services. It also seems a bit awkward to argue that people with a college degree—

who reaped huge wage gains in the 1980s and early 1990s—are suddenly doing routine work and hence experiencing stagnant earnings.

Whatever one thinks of the technological version of the polarization idea, it is simply not the case that there will be few new job openings for middle-skill work.[16] According to projections by the Bureau of Labor Statistics, only 23 percent of all job openings projected between 2008 and 2018 will require a college degree or more.[17] Examples of good jobs that are attainable with less than a four-year degree include numerous health care and biotechnology technician jobs, skilled blue-collar work, computer support jobs, and truck drivers. Other projections suggest that there will be a good number of new jobs available for skilled blue-collar work (machine maintenance, technicians, repair jobs, and the like) and that these too require education in the range of "some college" or an associate's degree. These projections are particularly likely in light of the upcoming need to hire replacements for the retiring generation of baby boomers. For example, while it is true that between 2008 and 2018 the total number of production workers in the economy is expected to decline, there will nonetheless be over 2.1 million new openings for production workers owing to replacement hiring.

Additional evidence on this point comes from the success of students who obtain an occupational credential from a community college. Community colleges account for about 45 percent of postsecondary credit enrollment as well as a large number of people taking noncredit, largely vocational courses. Public community college students do not resemble the traditional image of a college student. Nearly 40 percent are over age twenty-four, and 60 percent attend part-time. Indeed, the rhetoric regarding the diminishing importance of the traditional college student is really about community college students. Community college students are more likely to be minority, more likely to be self-supporting, and more likely to be first-generation college students. Over 15 percent of community college students are African American, and nearly 15 percent are Hispanic. Forty percent of community college students are the first generation in their family to attend college. Community colleges are heavily oriented toward occupational training, with more than half the students enrolled in explicitly occupational tracks. Students who obtain a credential, whether a certificate or an AA degree, do indeed find work, as is evidenced by studies that examine employment rates and wages.[18] A fly in the ointment is the very low completion rate in many community colleges, but a great deal of energy, both governmental and through foundations, is flowing toward addressing this problem. For our purposes here, the bottom line is that there are indeed good middle-skill jobs available.

Conclusion

There is no question that over the past several decades the skill levels demanded by firms have increased. Nor is there any question that there are many low-wage workers for whom more education and training would be very helpful in bettering their situation. Skills are an important part of the story of what is going wrong in the low-wage labor market, and we fully accept this point.

That being said, too much of the discussion revolves entirely around skills and education. There tends to be, at least among some scholars and policymakers, an almost learned blindness to seeing the problem in a broader frame. For example, the Congressional Budget Office (CBO), in a recent report on the low-wage labor market, wrote that in the 1990s the trajectory of the wage distribution was explainable by "changes in how employers value worker skills . . . factors such as motivation, intelligence, or specific educational or vocational background."[19] In making this statement, the CBO ignores not only the low explanatory power of the few statistical models that include a range of skill and behavioral traits but also the pervasive evidence that other factors are important. For example, the decline of the minimum wage in the 1980s and the weakening of unions explain much of the growth in earnings inequality during those years.[20] In addition, since the 1980s most of the shifts in the earnings distribution have come at the top. Efforts to explain this purely in terms of skill seem strained, to say the least.

The exclusive focus on skill is also problematic because of the time horizon implied by arguing that education and training is the dominant solution. The high returns to education that are commonly cited refer to the gains that an individual can expect, not to the gains that would accrue to millions of people if somehow schooling and training were increased very broadly. Such an increase in skill levels will take decades to affect the quality of jobs that firms offer. We cannot simply rely on education and training to upgrade the quality of jobs in the low-wage labor market. A first step toward a richer policy menu is to think more deeply about what drives firms as they make decisions about how to organize work, and this is the topic of the next chapter.

CHAPTER 4

How Firms Think

The Integrated Packaging Corporation runs a factory in New Brunswick, New Jersey, that produces corrugated boxes.[1] The plant's workforce is 60 percent minority, and the jobs of production workers are, at best, moderately skilled. In 2000, the poverty rate in the area was 38 percent and the unemployment rate 18 percent. In the plant itself, 50 percent of the hourly workers did not have a high school degree, and 75 percent were not native English speakers. Given these circumstances, it would not have been hard to drive wages down near the minimum. Yet despite all this, in the year 2000, the average W-2 for hourly workers at the plant was $50,000. At Integrated Packaging all employees, managers, and hourly workers receive the same benefits package. Hourly workers receive cross-training on a variety of machines, and about half of the hourly workers eventually manage to land salaried jobs in the plant. In weekly meetings, managers and the production staff share information about production issues and the financial circumstances of the firm. The quit rate is near zero.

This story shows that it is indeed possible to manage a business that runs against the grain and provides decent jobs in situations where the opposite expectation is more reasonable. Yet obviously Integrated Packaging is not the norm. How do firms think about organizing work, and what are the opportunities for moving them in the direction of higher-quality jobs?

Decisions about job quality lie with firms, and therefore we need to understand the pressures that firms face and how they make choices about organizing their work. Our view stands in contrast to the perspective that employer decision-making is a mechanical response to market signals. When an employer says (as many do), "We can't pay any better because we match the market, and if we did anything different we would lose our customers," that employer is expressing the economics textbook view of the firm as a passive price- and wage-taker and combining it with another common argument:

product markets will punish any firm that lets its costs drift above the market norm.

In reality, there is more to say about the employment practices of firms than just the view that they are helpless actors buffeted by market imperatives. Firms make choices about how to organize work, and these choices are driven by a range of considerations. It is possible to find firms in the same product and labor markets with quite different strategies for managing and organizing their workforces. The differences sometimes emerge from the values of the managers, and sometimes from a different understanding of the payoffs that can flow from a workforce that has reason to feel committed to the enterprise because the enterprise seems committed to its employees.

These different approaches are sometimes termed "high-road" and "low-road," which have the obvious normative implications. These terms emerged over a decade ago in the context of the debate over how America should respond to foreign competition. One view was that firms needed to obtain greater efficiencies by reducing employment-related costs as deeply as possible. The other view was that a firm's human capital was a key competitive asset and that investments in the workforce would pay off in terms of productivity and quality. While obviously these labels are much too simple, they do provide a handy way of capturing two broadly distinct strategies.

We take a somewhat different angle on the question. Our perspective on firms in the low-wage labor market might be termed "tough love." We begin by insisting that firms have choices about how to organize work. We offer examples of employers that produce the same goods and services provided by most low-wage employers yet whose jobs are of noticeably higher quality than the norm. This comparison, of course, raises the question of why other firms do not follow this model, and here we offer a different view than is common among most scholars and advocates who write on this topic. We believe that many high-road employers, if not most of them, are idiosyncratic in ways that sharply distinguish them from the average employer. The fact is that most low-wage employers find themselves in intensely competitive markets in which squeezing their employees appears to be the only viable survival strategy. Although some firms, such as Wal-Mart or high-end hotels and restaurants, may have healthy margins that should enable them to treat their employees better, we think that this is not the norm.

There may well be gains from treating employees better—and we believe that there are—but these gains do not appear to be worth the costs in the eyes of most firms. That this is true is demonstrated by some discouraging international comparisons. Even in countries where the overall economy provides a much higher degree of equality than is the case in the United States, the organization of work in industries such as retail and hotels is very similar to ours. Put most starkly, the low road appears to be the most sensible and profitable path for most organizations. With this perspective in mind, we de-

Table 4.1   Industry Distribution of Low-Wage Work, 2010

	Percentage of Low-Wage Workers Found in This Industry	Percentage of Workers in This Industry Who Are Low-Wage
Retail trade	18.9%	44.6%
Food and drink	12.4	72.9
Health	10.7	20.5
Manufacturing	8.7	17.5
Education	7.0	14.8
Administration and support services	6.7	45.1
Construction	4.1	17.9
Social assistance	3.9	43.2
Accommodations	2.4	54.7
Arts, entertainment, recreation	2.6	34.9
Personal and laundry services	2.1	65.2
Agriculture	1.8	7.3
Public administration	1.8	7.4
Private household	0.5	61.8

Source: Authors' calculations. See chapter 1 appendix for further information on data sources.

scribe the employment practices, such as contracting out, that have put downward pressure on job quality in the low-wage labor market.

In thinking about how to improve job quality, we return to the earlier point that there are benefits to be reaped by following the high road. The policy challenge is to both prod and assist firms in adopting this strategy. At the same time, we also need to recognize that these are not easy choices and that, at least from the firm's perspective, which does not include social costs, the benefits do not always offset the costs. The chapter concludes by laying the groundwork for the discussion of these issues in the policy chapters that follow.

Profiling the Low-Wage Job Market

Where are low-wage jobs located? Which patterns of employment will help us think about how to improve the quality of work? In table 4.1, we begin to answer these questions by examining the industries where most low-wage workers are found. In the first column, we show the percentage of all workers in below-standard jobs found in a given industry, and in the second column

Table 4.2   Employees Compensated Below Standard, by Occupation, 2010

	Percentage of All Below-Standard Employees in This Occupation	Percentage of Employees in This Occupation in Below-Standard Jobs
Office and administration	13.8%	23.9%
Sales and related services	13.5	36.9
Food preparation and service	13.1	74.1
Buildings and grounds, cleaning and maintenance	8.5	58.7
Transportation and material-moving	8.4	34.7
Production	8.2	30.1
Personal care and service	6.4	60.7
Education, training, library	4.7	14.9
Health care support	4.7	46.8

Source: Authors' calculations. See chapter 1 appendix for further information on data sources.

we show the fraction of all workers in that industry who have below-standard jobs. The industries represented in this table account for 84 percent of all low-wage work.

The table shows that some industries, such as retail and food serving, account for a substantial fraction of all low-wage employees and are also fundamentally low-wage industries in the sense that the jobs of a large fraction of their employees fall below the standard. On the other hand, health care and manufacturing are not low-wage industries, since relatively few workers in these sectors receive low pay, but because of their large size they nonetheless account for a substantial fraction of low-wage work. The difference between retail and food, on the one hand, and health and manufacturing, on the other, would seem to be that improving the circumstances of low-wage work in retail involves a much broader transformation of the industry's way of organizing itself than is the case in health care or manufacturing. Of course, an examination of more textured distinctions makes some manufacturing industries—say, textiles, or health care industries such as nursing homes—begin to look like retail or food service in their distribution of work.

The other insight from these data is that some industries that are frequently discussed in the policy literature, such as hotels or laundries or personal service, account for a very small fraction of all low-wage work even though they are clearly low-wage industries in the sense that most employees are compensated poorly.

Table 4.2 goes through the same exercises, this time classifying employees

Figure 4.1   Percentage of Employees Below Standard, by Industry Characteristics, 2010

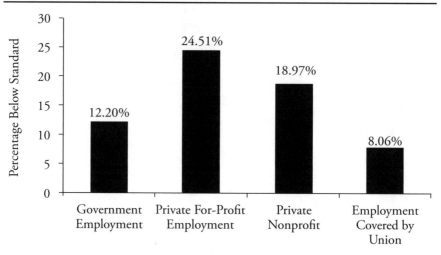

Source: Authors' calculations. See chapter 1 appendix for further details on data sources.

by their occupation. Only occupations whose low-wage employees count for 5 percent or more of the low-wage population are included in the table (with the exception of health care, which comes close to 5 percent and which is the subject of great many policy interventions).

These occupations together account for 82 percent of all workers in be-low-standard jobs. Whereas, in the past, poverty was associated with agricultural work and grinding factory jobs, today many low-wage workers are found in service and white-collar jobs. Indeed, the prominence of administrative work in these data is a surprise.

The importance of the organizational characteristics of the job itself is obvious in figure 4.1. Government employment is much less likely than private-sector work to be below standard. This pattern is a bit deceptive, however, since the low rate of below-standard work applies to people who are directly employed in the public sector. A great many other low-wage workers—for example, those in health and education services—work for organizations that depend heavily on public funding. This distinction proves important when it comes to thinking about policy, and so the patterns shown here should not be interpreted as letting the government off the hook for job quality.

This figure also demonstrates that if a job is covered by a union, the chances that it will be below standard fall dramatically. Interpreting this pattern is a little tricky: it may be due to unions being in high-wage industries (such as the auto industry), or it may be that unions change basic conditions

Table 4.3   Firm Size and Below-Standard Work, 2007

	Distribution of All Employees	Employees in Each Size Category Who Fall Below Standard	Distribution of Workers in Below-Standard Jobs
Less than 25 employees	20.5%	40.1%	33.1%
25 to 99 employees	13.6	27.9	15.4
100 to 499 employees	15.1	22.3	13.6
500 employees or more	50.6	18.4	37.7
Total	100		100

Source: Authors' calculations. See chapter 1 appendix for further information on data sources.
Note: Data refer to civilian wage and salary employees between the ages of twenty-five and sixty-four.

of work in traditional low-wage sectors (for example, the improvements that unions in Las Vegas have made for hotel room cleaners). Of course, the historical record clearly shows that when unions started in previously unorganized industries (again, such as autos) they improved wages and working conditions, and so the concern about the direction of causality should not be too worrying. We return in chapter 6 to a discussion of the role of employee representation in improving job quality.

A final key question is explored in table 4.3: the relationship between firm size and work quality. As the first column shows, over half of all employees are in very large firms, while only about 20 percent are in the smallest. However, the risk of working below standard is much higher in small firms than in large ones. Forty percent of employees in the smallest firms occupy below-standard jobs, while the figure is less than half that in the largest firms. Again, however, the rate of risk has to be combined with the size of the risk pool in order to see where the highest numbers of people in difficulty are located. The final column shows that, while one-third of workers in below-standard jobs work in the smallest firms, slightly more than that are employed in the very largest firms. Put differently, it is clear that any overall strategy must address the special difficulties facing small employers, while not letting large enterprises off the hook.

Thinking About Firms

How should we think about firms in the low-wage labor market? One approach is to focus on bad behavior, and in particular on violations of labor standards such as the minimum wage and overtime laws. In this view, improved enforcement is a key policy goal. We agree that employment standards violations are widespread, and in chapter 5 we take up this question in detail. Indeed, some firms think of labor standards violations as a routine element of their human resource practices. But in general we do not think that this is the most fruitful way to think about the problems of employers in the low-wage labor market.

Why do we think that enforcing current standards would not solve the problem? Consider the findings from one of the most comprehensive studies available of employment law violations. In an innovative project, a network of researchers in New York, Chicago, and Los Angeles surveyed frontline (nonmanagerial, nonprofessional, and nontechnical) employees in industries such as restaurants and home health care.[2] The survey uncovered widespread violations; indeed, a shocking 68 percent of all the employees captured by the survey had lost some earnings in the previous year due to minimum wage, overtime, or other violations. But what would a resolution of this problem mean? If employees in the sample had received all of the wages and benefits to which they were legally entitled, their average earnings would have been $17,616 instead of the $14,982 they actually received. The gap is far from trivial, but, had it been eliminated, these employees would still have been well below any reasonable standard for decent work.

Enforcing standards at their current level would not bring wages and other employment conditions anywhere near the level we consider appropriate, but before we talk seriously about raising standards (as we will), it is important to understand the pressures on firms, the choices they think they face, and how they make decisions regarding the organization of employment. In other words, we want to take a nuanced look at the problems of employers.

The High-Road/Low-Road Story and Its Problems

To anyone outside of academia, it obviously makes a difference where one works. Everyone knows that there are good employers and bad employers. Magazines publish lists of the one hundred best firms, and when students leave high school or college and compare job offers, there is a clear pecking order about who landed in the best places.

Economists think about this in a different way. The question is whether, within the same labor market, and after holding constant the skills and other personal attributes of an employee, it makes a difference where that person works. The point is that, if markets function well, then two high school graduates who have the same skills and other capacities should have broadly similar pay if they work in the same area. This is true because of the behavior of firms. Given the available technology and the going market wages for employees at different skill levels, all firms should optimize in the same way by paying the market wage and organizing their work in the most cost-efficient manner. After taking into account so-called nonpecuniary factors, such as prestige or cleanliness, considerations that are offset by wage differences, it should not make any difference where an employee works.

We begin by agreeing with the common view that there is choice—that some firms do in fact offer better jobs than do others operating within the same product and labor markets. There are, as many people concerned with these issues like to argue, high-road firms. It is important to acknowledge this point, both because there is truth to it and because it has played such an important part in the debate and the rhetoric around improving job quality. But the second part of our story is darker. Most high-road firms are idiosyncratic in ways that defy generalization to the larger universe of employers. Most firms in the low-wage labor market are under such intense competitive pressure that they see few alternatives to squeezing their workforce. This is the reality with which we must contend. But first, what is the evidence of choice?

Researchers working with nationally representative surveys that include information on both employees and the firms in which they work have shown that, after controlling for the education of the workforce (education being the only measure of skill that is typically measured in these data sets), substantial variation remains in pay practices among firms in the same industry.[3] The difficulty, of course, is that with only education held constant there is always the possibility that the pay differences among employers reflect different skill mixes in their labor forces. Concerns of this kind can never be eliminated, but the pattern of findings from different data sets is consistent enough to make it very likely that the finding is valid.

The more commonly cited evidence of high-road practices draws on examples of firms that implement employment practices that seem well above the norm for their industry. Our earlier example of Integrated Packaging is typical, and there are other examples. Susan Eaton studied the nursing home industry and identified employers that paid above-average wages, provided mobility options for their nursing assistants, and garnered considerably better resident satisfaction than did their competitors.[4] The Hitachi Foundation and the Public Health Institute have published cases of other high-road long-term care facilities.[5] A famous Harvard Business School case describes the practices of ServiceMaster, a large national janitorial services firm that provides high levels of training to its employees and pays wages that are well above average. And Costco is widely cited for paying above-average wages to its retail workers, wages that look good particularly in comparison to Wal-Mart.[6]

These cases are important because they provide what might be termed "existence proofs": it is possible to run a business in a low-wage industry with higher employment standards than is the norm. However, it is a long and very uncertain step to a conclusion that the typical firm can follow this path. It turns out on closer examination that most of the examples widely cited are unusual in important ways. The high-road nursing homes tend to be run by religious or ethnic groups that are willing to accept a lower rate of return to serve their members. ServiceMaster was owned by a deeply religious man who organized the firm to follow his beliefs (hence the name, which comes from "Serve Your Master"), but the nature of the company changed when it was sold to a private equity firm. Similarly, Costco is owned by a person with strong personal beliefs about how to treat employees. In short, there is typically something distinctive and not generalizable about the high-road examples. The main exception to this point is the unionized firm in a low-wage industry. In some sense, however, this also is a distinctive case. (We return to the role of unions in a subsequent chapter.) What, then, is the typical circumstance of firms in the low-wage labor market?

THE COMPETITIVE ENVIRONMENT

The changes in the environment facing firms have been breathtaking. Consider a bookseller facing Amazon, an established airline facing Southwest Airlines, a dry cleaner facing Zoots, a technology firm facing the start-ups in the Silicon Valley, a retailer facing Wal-Mart, General Motors facing Toyota. The list could go on and on. When the environment of the American icon Kodak was turned upside down by digital photography, employment fell from 145,000 in 1988 to 20,000 in 2009.

The competitive landscape has gotten tougher for a variety of reasons. In some industries—transportation, telecommunications, and banking to name a few—deregulation has forced enterprises to compete much more seriously than in the past. However, deregulation is not the only source of more competitive markets, and throughout the economy the range of competitors has expanded greatly. Some of the new competitors have been from overseas: the value of imports as a percentage of GDP has more than tripled over the past several decades.[7] However, much of the new competition is purely domestic as new firms have emerged to challenge incumbents in a variety of industries. Throughout this period, product cycles have shortened, customers have become more demanding, and formerly standardized markets have fragmented into niches.

The foregoing is about the economy as a whole, and in particular the circumstances confronting large, well-established enterprises. There is every reason to think that the firms occupying the low-wage labor market face similar, if not more difficult, competitive pressures. First, consider the small-firm sector in general; this group of employers, as we have seen, account for about one-third of low-wage employment. Life for small employers is brutal: about 40 percent of all small-business jobs disappear within six years after beginning, and between three and four out of every five small-business firms close within five years of opening.[8] Recent research shows that while small firms do create slightly more jobs than would be expected given their share of overall employment, they also experience above-average rates of job destruction.[9]

Examining the situation in specific industries gives us a closer view of the challenges of low-wage firms. Retail is the easiest to look at, because everyone knows about the impact of Wal-Mart. Wal-Mart drives down wages and forces its competitors to shrink or go out of business. (There are also upsides to Wal-Mart, which are discussed later in the book.) Although it is difficult to present a clean counterfactual (what would wages be were there no Wal-Mart?), researchers are able to examine the impact on local retail wages when a new Wal-Mart opens in a community. Using sophisticated techniques to control for the possibility that Wal-Mart chooses low-wage communities in which to open stores (and hence the link between a Wal-Mart and local wages would be an artifact), two independent studies have reached the same conclusion: when a Wal-Mart opens in a location, retail wages in that area fall. One study found that when ten Wal-Marts are opened in a state, retail wages fall by 2 percent. Since the average number of stores per state is seventy-six, retail earnings are 15 percent below what they would be without Wal-Mart.[10] Other researchers find similar patterns using national data.[11] And in a local example, there is evidence that after two Wal-Mart supercenters opened in Houston, sales at a nearby Kroger's dropped 10 percent and worker hours fell by 30 to 40 percent.[12]

The impact of these pressures can be seen in a set of eighteen case studies of food and electronics retailers.[13] The researchers summarized their findings as follows:

> All companies in our sample espoused cost-cutting strategies, and almost all sought as well to improve services and product quality. . . . For virtually all companies, the goals of cost-cutting and improving service and quality are in tension, and at times in conflict. . . . The fact that cost-cutting often undermines job quality—because labor costs are the "number one controllable" cost in stores—is a key dimension of these tensions and conflicts. . . . "With competition like Wal-Mart," said a district HR manager at [one store], "it's difficult to pay our employees a higher wage while maintaining competitiveness." [Another manager said,] "Only the people at the top of the scale got . . . progressive increases. People in the lower ranks were frozen. That's a huge, huge, huge change from what they're used to. They're used to seeing a 3, 4% increase every year of the contract." (2)

Another example of the intense pressures faced by low-wage firms is provided by David Weil's study of the franchising of building cleaning services.[14] Cleaning franchise operations tend to be large—for example, one national firm, Coverall, had 5,400 franchises in 2008—and have become increasingly more common. From his careful examination of the nature of the franchise contracts, in all of which the brand-name firm required the franchisee to pay very substantial fees, Weil concluded that it was not possible to make money without paying employees the minimum wage or below.

In yet another low-wage industry, hotels, the competitive landscape is also very difficult. Top chains account for only 58 percent of total rooms, and even that figure is too high because in many cases the chain has simply sold its brand to a property owner.[15] Pressure on costs are intense, and with over half of all employment accounted for by housekeepers and other cleaning staff, low-wage labor is the main target. Squeezing the workforce is one of the few available strategies for increasing profit margins.

The health care sector is another large low-wage employer under considerable competitive pressure. Nursing homes are under obvious pressures given the extremely labor-intensive nature of the business and the limited opportunities for price increases due to the sector's reliance on publicly paid reimbursements. However, there are also considerable pressures in hospitals, another large employer of low-wage labor. The hospital industry is highly fragmented—the top fifty organizations deliver only 30 percent of total revenue[16]—and it faces additional competition from stand-alone providers such as imaging centers and endoscopy suites as well as specialty hospitals. The American Hospital Association reports that 30 percent of hospitals lose money.[17] Although a great deal of remarkably sophisticated technology is at work in hospitals, labor still accounts for 40 percent of costs.[18] The majority of the workforce consists of frontline employees: nurses, technicians, orderlies, kitchen staff. Given these circumstances, it is perhaps not surprising, but nonetheless striking, that a recent analysis of the industry by McKinsey described it in the same terms that have been used to describe a discount retail chain trying to survive against Wal-Mart.[19]

The Instability of the High Road and How to Remedy It

The fate of two union partnerships in classic low-wage industries—the agreement between the garment union UNITE and Levi Strauss, and the San Francisco Hotels Partnership—illustrates this sad story line.

In a very tough industry, Levi Strauss had long stood out as a firm willing to go the extra mile to improve the quality of jobs for its low-wage employees. Levi Strauss's decision to go private in the 1980s created favorable conditions by relieving stock market pressure, and in the mid-1990s the firm reached an agreement with the union that included a degree of power-sharing, the introduction of team-based production, flexible work rules, and a level of job security stemming from the firm's commitment to continue producing in North America. Yet over time this agreement eroded. The firm

closed a large number of plants in the late 1990s, and eventually it com-
pletely stopped producing in the United States. Neither genuine social commitment nor innovative work systems could protect the firm or its employees
against the pressure of low-wage competition.

As compelling as this case may be, it is easy to see it as an extreme because
the apparel industry is extremely vulnerable to overseas threats. It is often said
that domestic service industries can avoid such a fate because their work has
to be done onshore. However, the case of the San Francisco hotels raises some
doubt about this optimism. As already discussed at several points, hotels employ large numbers of low-wage workers in housekeeping, kitchen, laundry,
and other service jobs. In many major markets, at least some of the leading
hotels are unionized, and for some of those properties, innovative agreements—such as in Las Vegas and to a lesser extent in Boston—have opened
up better career opportunities for employees. A model that attracted national
attention was a 1994 multi-hotel agreement in San Francisco between the
union HERE and a consortium of eleven high-end hotels. The first contract,
which ran until 1999 and was renewed in 2004, was regarded as a model of
win-win bargaining. In return for flexibility in staffing, job definitions, and
work rules, the employees received a large training fund, a unified hiring hall
to create opportunities for upward mobility, a gain-sharing plan that linked
wage increases to productivity, and participation in problem-solving groups.[20]
In assessing this achievement, the employment lawyer representing the hotels
wrote: "If any union and management group can find a real solution to tough
issues it is the San Francisco Hotel Partnership with its years of successful
experience with interest based problem solving."[21]

Today the agreement has fallen apart, and the unions are striking several
hotels and have placed ten hotels under boycott. Good feelings and cooperation, not to mention wage gains and career ladders, are long gone. What happened? The hotels pushed for increased employee contributions to health insurance, for wage reductions, and for workload increases. The justification
was increased competition from non-union hotels. The union responded by
pointing to high occupancy rates and profitability in the tourist-heavy San
Francisco market. The point here is not to judge the merits of either side's
arguments, but rather to observe that a state-of-the-art accommodation in a
classic low-wage industry was unable to survive the pressures it confronted.

The fragility of high-road employment practices is not limited to agreements with unions. Recall the case of ServiceMaster, the firm portrayed in a
well-known business school case as exemplary in its treatment of janitors.
When a private equity company took over, all that changed. Another example is provided by the high-end retail firms, such as Circuit City, that tried to
compete on the basis of service quality and did so by paying salespeople well
above the rates of competitors such as Wal-Mart. Yet, precisely under pres-

sure from Wal-Mart, these firms reversed course, laid off the skilled sales-people and reduced training, and went the cheap labor route.[22] Consider also the nursing home we described in the first chapter, the facility that offers its CNAs training and opportunities for promotions to licensed practical nurse positions. The darker side of this story is that the program is funded by a philanthropist who believes in it, not out of the operating budget of the nursing home. The staff fear that without this outside support the nursing home would stop offering its low-paid workers these opportunities.

It's the Same Across the Sea

Additional evidence of the relentless pressure on firms, and the consequences of this pressure for job quality, comes from examining trends in low-wage industries in Europe. Russell Sage Foundation researchers studied how work is organized and compensated in classic low-wage industries such as retail, hotels, health care, and food manufacturing.[23] The core finding was that competitive pressures pushed firms toward squeezing their employees as much as legally possible.

For retail jobs in food sales, 35 percent of American employees were paid below the same low-wage standard that we have been using, compared to 26 percent in France, 29 percent in Germany and Denmark, and 57 percent in the Netherlands. The researchers concluded that "retail jobs have gotten worse across the countries in our sample."[24] For hotels, the "surprising finding" was that "room attendants in all six countries appear to be working right at the bottom of their respective labor markets."[25] It is true that in both of these industries there are some shadings to the pattern. For example, union contracts and governmental regulation often give employees more control over schedules in European nations than is possible in the United States. In Germany, retail clerks have broader and more interesting work because of the nation's strong vocational training system, which gives them more extensive skills than is the case in other nations. However, the core point is that wages have been driven down across all countries in these industries. It is worth noting that the story line is more optimistic in health care in that nursing assistants receive relatively better wages in most of the continental European nations than they do in the United States. It is also notable, however, that the situation is rapidly deteriorating in Germany as more jobs are outsourced to firms that provide worse jobs, the doctors' union has ceased to cooperate with unions representing low-wage workers, and the federal states have withdrawn from national contracts.

A second, more subtle finding emerging from this project is that there is very little evidence in Europe of differences across firms in the same industry—that is, evidence that some employers have successfully taken the high road. Indeed, in the hotel research, the core finding is that even chains that emphasize very high standards of customer service squeeze their employees just as much as hotels lower down the quality hierarchy. Evidently, high-quality business strategy does not translate into better conditions for employees.

The Consequences of Pressure: How Firms Respond

The stress of competition in low-wage industries obviously leads firms to do everything they can to limit labor costs, for the simple reason that compensation, they feel, is among their most controllable costs. When there are adequate supplies of workers who are willing—or better said, needing—to work at low wages, then squeezing pay is feasible.

EMPLOYMENT LAW VIOLATION AS A STRATEGY

One tactic that does not show up in human resource management textbooks—but nonetheless must be considered a conscious response to competitive pressure—is to violate the law. In many ways the poster child of this strategy has been Wal-Mart: there is a great deal of evidence that the firm has systematically evaded employment law by forcing its hourly staff to work off the clock—that is, to work extra hours without receiving overtime pay. The firm has lost a series of court decisions, but even more compelling is testimony that the core employment model enforced by corporate headquarters is pressuring store managers to squeeze labor.[26] Store managers are monitored (twice a week!) by Wal-Mart headquarters on their payroll costs as a percentage of sales and given a target to meet. Managerial salaries depend on reaching that target, and overtime costs are neither assumed nor even exist in the model's calculation. By contrast, there is no equivalent monitoring of labor practices. In the words of an expert who examined these practices as part of one of the lawsuits: "A store manager would have to be very dense to miss the signal—financial and business targets are very important at Wal-Mart, and compliance with regulations and policies with respect to employees is very much less important."[27]

Wal-Mart may get the most attention in the media, but employment law violations appear to be relatively common throughout the low-wage labor market. Researchers in New York State found that 67 percent of domestic workers receive no overtime pay, 59 percent of restaurant employees have the same problem, and small retail stores in Brooklyn routinely violate wage and hour laws. Nor were these behaviors the result of only a few bad apples. A network of employment brokers and storefront employment agencies systematically recruited and placed people in jobs in which violations were common.[28] Other geographically specific case studies have found similar patterns;

for example, in the Phoenix area, widespread overtime violations were found among contractors working for the nation's largest homebuilder.[29] A recent review of the national literature concluded that the evidence suggests that 50 percent of day laborers suffer wage theft, that 60 percent of nursing homes are out of compliance, and that nearly 100 percent of poultry plants violate wage and hour laws.[30] Recall also the three-city survey mentioned earlier that found that 68 percent of all the employees captured by the survey had lost some earnings over the course of the previous year owing to minimum wage, overtime, or other violations.[31] Surveys of employees in other regions reach similar conclusions.[32]

In addition to violations of the Fair Labor Standards Act, misclassification of employees also appears to be widespread. According to the U.S. Department of Labor, employers can reduce their labor cost expenses between 20 and 40 percent by misclassifying employees as independent contractors.[33] It is not hard to see the compelling incentive to misclassify employees in highly competitive low-wage and low-margin industries.

An audit of employers in nine states, conducted for the Department of Labor in 2000, found that between 10 and 30 percent of all employers had misclassified some workers.[34] In 2009, a commission appointed by the governor of Michigan reported that on average 30 percent of employers in the construction industry had misclassified workers as self-employed or had underreported payroll for UI tax and workers' compensation purposes.[35] In New York, grocery delivery workers were treated by their employers as independent contractors and made less than $2 an hour. They sued their employers as well, and workers in one case settled for $3 million in back pay.[36] In recent years, the attorneys general of California, Connecticut, Massachusetts, New York, and Ohio have aggressively sued employers for misclassifying employees.[37]

LEGAL RESPONSES TO COMPETITIVE PRESSURE

Employment law violations are a big problem, and we will address regulatory strategies in a subsequent chapter. But it would be a mistake to think that legal concerns are the most serious issue in the low-wage job market. Most employers, including most low-wage employers, obey the law, and even if one were to doubt this, it is unquestionable that even perfect compliance would not change the fact that wages are still too low and employment too precarious. For this reason, it is important to look in more detail at some of the strategies that employers have adopted to push down wages, including extensive subcontracting, greater use of independent contractors, and tough restrictions on any investments in their employees' skills.

Firms contract out for a variety of reasons, but an important one is to reduce the wage costs of a particular activity by removing the employees from the firm's own compensation structure. This creates a situation in which contractors compete for business in part on the basis of wage costs. This strategy can be very advantageous when a firm's internal compensation system pushes wages up for all occupations. Classic examples of this are building cleaners and security guards. A second cost-related motivation for subcontracting is to avoid legal liability for benefits and federal regulations (such as overtime) by having someone else be responsible for the employees.

How common is this practice? Anecdotal evidence suggests that it is widespread. Recall the discussion of the Hyatt Hotel room cleaners. This was a classic example of forcing down wages by expelling the employees from the firm and turning the function over to a contractor. The school board of Newton, Massachusetts, proposed privatizing the work of cafeteria workers to save on wage costs.[38] These examples can be multiplied many times over, but when it comes to nationally representative data, things get tricky because of the variety of forms the practice can take. Sometimes firms use temporary help firms as their subcontractor, and sometimes the subcontracting firm is a permanent employer of employees in the particular occupation. It is possible to get reasonable data on temp firms, but in the latter scenario it is very hard to know which firms are subcontracting for jobs previously done in-house. That being said, evidence from a variety of sources suggests that the use of temporary and contracted-out workers has grown very substantially in the past two decades.[39]

How do we know that wages and working conditions are worsened as a result of subcontracting? Strong evidence comes from a study that examined two occupations, security guards and janitors.[40] Using census data, the authors found that the share of janitors who were outsourced grew from 16 percent to 22 percent between 1983 and 2000 and for security guards the share grew from 40 percent to 50 percent. Furthermore, the rate of outsourcing grew most rapidly in high-wage industries. The wage differential between outsourced and in-house employees was $1.33 an hour for janitors and $2.34 for security jobs, and these differentials changed only slightly when controls were introduced for human capital. In addition, health care coverage was substantially less likely for outsourced employees than for in-house employees. The researchers concluded that, "overall, outsourcing appears to have altered the wage distribution by taking mid-to-high paying jobs and turning them into lower paying ones."[41]

Additional evidence on the impact of subcontracting comes from a study of employees at the San Francisco Airport.[42] In the course of investigating the impact of a living wage ordinance, researchers collected wage data on regular and outsourced employees in the same occupation. They found that the average wage for a regular customer service worker was $11.25 an hour in 1998, compared to $8.00 for a contract worker doing the same job; a regular ramp worker received $12.10 an hour compared to the $7.10 that a subcontracted employee got; and for cabin cleaners the wages were $10.80 and $7.20 an hour, respectively.

In yet another study, this one using a different source of data and examining a broader range of occupations, the authors concluded: "Evidence suggests that contract employment is associated with lower job security, as manifested through decreased job tenure and reduced opportunities for advancement."[43] Finally, case studies of subcontracting in three industries (auto suppliers, hospitals, and public schools) concluded that "adverse effects are clearest when . . . low skill workers in an organization receive relatively high compensation, and when employers are not blocked from substituting these employees with agency temporaries or contract workers."[44]

It is also worth noting that all of these conclusions are probably underestimates of the impact of outsourcing on wages because they ignore the threat effect. Employees are much less likely to push for higher compensation if they worry that this will lead their employers to spin off their jobs.

LIMITED TRAINING

Another strategy of low-wage employers is to save money by limiting investment in the skills of their employees. Good data on training inside firms are hard to find, but table 4.4 tells the basic story. Employees with low levels of education receive far less training than do their better-educated colleagues, and in the same vein, low-paid employees receive much less training than do better-paid workers. These practices represent savings for employers and to some extent may be reasonable in that workers with low-skill jobs presumably need less training to do their work than do employees with more complex tasks. However, the paucity of training also reflects a state of mind—the assumption that some workers simply cannot learn and that improvements in the quality of their work or their career trajectories are not feasible. Typical is the observation of an evaluation team that interviewed firms participating in a set of activities organized by the National Association of Manufacturers (NAM), with the intention of helping them upgrade their production practices: "Employers knew they had problems of absenteeism, turnover, skill deficiencies, and low productivity but accepted them fatalistically as 'facts of life,' feeling that not much could be done about them."[45]

Shifting Firm Behavior

It seems apparent that, left to their own devices, most employers in the low-wage labor market continue to push wages down as low as labor supply permits. Just as standard economics predicts, the floor on wages is what they have to pay in order to attract an adequate supply of workers. There is little reason for firms to pay anything more than this, and as we have seen, the intense competitive pressures under which most firms operate provide a strong incentive to minimize labor costs. Added to this is limited managerial capac-

Table 4.4   Employees Receiving Employer-Provided Training, 1995 and 2001

	1995	2001
High school degree or less	22.2%	19.8%
Some college	44.1	44.5
Bachelor's degree or higher	50.0	54.1
Lowest earnings quintile	27.1	22.0
Next earnings quintile	31.3	33.7
Next highest earnings quintile	42.1	46.7
Highest earnings quintile	49.3	48.8

Source: Authors' calculations based on data from Mikelson and Nightingale (2004).

ity to consider any alternative strategy for organizing work, as well as risk aversion regarding any shift to a different employment regime.

A commonsensical way to think about this is to imagine going into a small or medium-size retailer or health care provider or hotel and trying to start a conversation with the manager about raising wages. The carrot you can offer the manager is this: if he or she compensates people better, they will respond by providing better-quality service and being less likely to leave, and hence the costs of the additional compensation can be offset (as we show momentarily). How will the manager react?

The first point is that, as a practical matter, it will be very hard to even get the manager's attention. He or she will be totally stretched out running the business and will have very little time to engage in the conversation. But pretend that you get past this barrier. In all likelihood, the manager will say that raising wages would make prices go up and then competitors would eat the firm's lunch. Margins are just too tight to even contemplate this policy. But what about the benefits that might accrue to offset these costs? The problem, from the manager's perspective, is that these benefits seem speculative and, in any case, unlikely to offset the total cost of the wage increase. Furthermore, the benefits accrue slowly over time, but the cost increase is immediate and very dangerous to the firm's survival. The risk is just not worth it, and even if the manager wanted to, there is no time to engage in experimentation. Finally, to make the conversation even more problematic, if this enterprise is part of a larger organization—a branch store, for example—the manager is probably being judged on margins on a weekly or monthly basis and finds the risks of any upward shifts in compensation too scary to even contemplate. In short, this conversation is going nowhere.

There are academic theories that dress this scenario up in complex models. Firms tend to follow what is termed "path dependence"—that is, they do not deviate very much from how they have always done things. Managers engage in local searches for solutions; they "muddle through" and do not seek out global optimums; and since managerial capacity is limited, they "satisfice" instead of trying to do the very best thing.[46] The time horizons of managers are shorter than might be considered optimum because of their own career concerns and risk aversion. All of this adds up to the same conclusion: the conversation is a nonstarter.

The implication of these facts of life is that it will take a shock to change patterns of behavior. In some cases the shock comes from competitors. U.S. auto firms did not change how they organized themselves or managed their employees until Japanese competitors dramatically cut into their markets by implementing a new human resource system that generated much higher quality at lower cost.[47] Such a competitive shock seems unlikely for most low-wage employers. Instead, the shock will have to come from either public policy or employee voice. How firms respond after the shock is administered will be the next question, and this opens a different avenue for public policy: helping firms improve their practices so that that can afford to raise the standards for their low-wage employees.

The idea here is that some combination of public policy and private institutions, such as unions, can constrain firms from following the low-wage strategy that comes naturally. In contrast to the standard prediction that constraints are inevitably costly, however, these constraints can have beneficial effects for employers by forcing them to invent new ways of doing business that, perhaps to their surprise, turn out in the long run to be more productive than their previous path. This idea emerged from the political economy literature.[48] In this view, the benefits are seen to come in the long run when firms and the overall economy shift to fundamentally different trajectories, but here we take a shorter-run view of what is possible. This point was anticipated in the 1950s by the notion of a "union shock effect." A firm that is unionized against its will often responds by finding more efficient ways to do business to offset the additional costs that it faces from the union. The shock of unionization forces the firm out of the inertia and risk-adverse behavior that we have discussed and can lead to a more productive path. For our purposes, this suggests a policy framework that limits firms' capacity to follow a labor-squeezing strategy and instead provides some assistance to them in finding ways to do well given these constraints.

Some Evidence

All of these ideas run up against a standard economics assumption that firms know best and are maximizing efficiency. Pick up an economics textbook and you will read that employers optimize their production and service delivery systems, taking into account the available technology and the prices of different inputs, including labor. The market drives them to this optimal point because firms that fail to reach it will not be able to survive against their lower-cost competitors. From this perspective, there is very little that can be done to upgrade firms because they are already doing the best they can. However, the evidence of one's own eyes as well as more sophisticated economic thinking show that this viewpoint is wrong.

Everyone who has been connected to organizations—and that means all of us—can easily think of times when it has been obvious that matters could have been arranged more efficiently. Research supports these impressions. Two economists, Nicholas Bloom and John Van Reenen, systematically surveyed small and medium-size firms across a wide range of countries regarding their management practices.[49] Their measures of management practices included indicators such as compensation policy and investments in training. The surveys covered both developed and developing countries; although the overall quality of management was higher in the richer nations, even in those, including the United States, there was substantial dispersion, with many firms scoring poorly. In other words, there was ample room for improvement.

Another way of determining whether any of this makes sense is to ask about the evidence that improving the circumstances of employees can pay off for the firm. It turns out that there is a good deal of research on this question, and the answer is encouraging.

Why should we expect that firms as well as employees would benefit from higher wages and more progressive employment practices? The reasons are relatively straightforward and operate via several channels. One explanation is turnover, which is costly to firms in terms of lost investment in training, recruitment and hiring expenses, and the costs associated with reduced productivity while new employees learn the job. Every human resource management (HRM) textbook makes these points, and the professional HRM literature is full of discussions regarding how to reduce turnover. To the extent that turnover is reduced by progressive employment practices—and the evidence we review in the remainder of this chapter shows that it is—then the firm benefits.

The second channel is employee effort. In virtually all employment settings, employees have opportunities to work hard or to work less hard, to put extra care into their work or to not be careful in their work, to treat customers well or to treat them badly. These behaviors are discretionary, and no amount of management monitoring or discipline can fully control them. The choices that employees make can have substantial impacts on product quality, productivity, and customer satisfaction, and in turn these choices are affected by the quality of the employment relationship.

These points may seem reasonable in principle, but are they true in practice? And in particular, are they true in the low-wage labor market? As it turns out, a wide range of evidence supports them. First, consider turnover. It is commonsensical that if people are paid more, they stay longer on the job, and a staggering volume of economics literature on quits confirms this expectation. A study of home health care aides in Los Angeles found that a $1 increase in pay (from $8 an hour to $9 an hour) reduced turnover by seventeen percentage points. Adding health insurance reduced turnover by twenty-one percentage points.[50] Other studies of low-wage occupations reach similar conclusions. When wages were raised at the San Francisco Airport following passage of a living wage ordinance, turnover fell by 5 percent for ramp workers, by 25 percent for baggage handlers, and by 44 percent for cabin cleaners.

Are there costs associated with turnover in the low-wage labor market? The answer is yes. A study of frontline workers in health care (orderlies, home health aides, and other jobs at the bottom of the ladder) estimated the cost of losing and then replacing an employee to be in the $2,500 to $6,000 range, depending on whether the costs of bringing the new employee up to speed were included in the calculation.[51] Research conducted at the Cornell University Hotel School found that in the year 2000 the cost of replacing a line cook in Miami was just over $2,000, a gift store clerk over $3,000, a hotel room cleaner over $1,300, and a front desk worker just under $6,000.[52]

The benefits that flow from better jobs are not just reduced turnover but also better performance. In a survey of the San Francisco Airport employers, 35 percent reported an improvement in overall performance, 29 percent a reduction in absenteeism, 44 percent a reduction in disciplinary issues, and 45 percent an improvement in customer service.[53] The researchers studied whether these improvements were due to changes in the composition of the workforce and concluded that they were not—that is, the same workers simply did a better job after the pay increase.

Another industry that employs large numbers of low-wage workers is health care, and in this industry there is also good evidence that firms can benefit when they adopt progressive policies aimed at how they structure employment. A powerful example is the partnership between a coalition of unions and the Kaiser Permanente health system. In sharp contrast to the contentious relationship in some health care systems (for example, Yale's relationship with employees in New Haven), the Kaiser Permanente partnership was built up over a number of years and involved a wide range of employees in a variety of activities, such as problem-solving teams. Employee surveys show that workers believe that their employment situation improved as a result of the more positive relationship, and most relevant to the point being made here, the employer also benefited. A careful multi-year study of the partnership that collected outcome data on a variety of issues concluded: "Where the partnership was active it had a significant effect on reducing costs and . . . at least in one region where the data were available, improving clinical performance."[54] A simple example of how this played out was a 46 percent reduction in "accepted claim" injury rates among employees, which flowed in large measure from improvements in practices initiated by the problem-solving groups.[55]

There is similar evidence in other low-wage industries. For example, a study of call centers found higher productivity in those centers where employees were organized in teams and able to exercise higher levels of discretion.[56] In an industry at a very different end of the technology and skill spectrum, restaurants, research found a positive relationship between employee satisfaction and customer satisfaction.[57]

Conclusion

Low-wage firms are under intense competitive pressure and have responded by pushing down on wages and adopting a set of employment practices that intensify downward compensation trends. Can these responses be held in check or reversed? Answering this question requires that we step back and think about how firms make decisions. The framework we propose begins with the proposition that many employers that offer substandard jobs do so because of the intense competitive pressures they face and because they lack the internal managerial capacity to think about alternative employment strategies. Others (think Wal-Mart) are not lacking in internal capacity, but still do not see another road toward success. The idea of beneficial constraints proposes that policy be used to force firms in another direction while simultaneously assisting them in reaping the performance gains that can flow from such a move. Finally, we acknowledge that better job quality is not a free good. In the end, at least for some firms, the gains from treating their employees better will not fully offset the costs. We take up this challenge later in the book. Here it is important to note that the social costs of bad work demand that we be willing to pay this price.

CHAPTER 5

Employment Standards

America has a long history of insisting on a baseline of employment conditions. The Commonwealth of Massachusetts passed the nation's first child labor law in 1836; nearly two centuries later, standard setting is now as traditional in America as baseball. Beginning with the Progressive era, accelerating with the New Deal, and continuing to the present day (with the support of President George H.W. Bush for the Americans with Disabilities Act), a broad range of regulations have undergirded work. The best known are minimum wage and overtime rules; protections against discrimination based on race, gender, age, disability status, or sexual orientation; pension protection; and occupational health and safety protection.

Until the New Deal, the very idea that the government might intervene to shape the employment relationship was contested. Employers argued, and many judges agreed, that the free exchange of labor was no different than any other commercial transaction, and hence, while contracts could be enforced by state power, the actual terms of those agreements were of no legitimate concern to the government. This view was discredited during the New Deal in a formal way through Supreme Court decisions and more fundamentally through a broad public acceptance that the labor market is different than the market for commodities. Today the vast majority of Americans agree on the importance of ensuring that employees are treated according to minimally accepted standards. The polling results discussed in the first chapter and the success of numerous ballot initiatives to raise state minimum wages make it clear that this commitment continues. And as we saw in chapter 2, good solid economic theory supports the public perception that labor market standards are appropriate.

But if the case in principle for standards is long since settled, much remains in doubt when it comes to the low-wage job market. Existing standards (such as the minimum wage and overtime rules) have been poorly enforced in recent years, and rates of compliance are troubling. Furthermore, it is far from clear how best to improve enforcement given the inherently limited resources compared to the size of the job market. Adding to these limitations are changes in how work is organized—in particular the spread of outsourcing—that complicate the problem well beyond what the authors of the New Deal system envisioned. On top of all this, consider that if the current minimum wage were perfectly enforced and compliance was 100 percent, many people would still be working at $7.25 an hour, well below what we consider minimally acceptable.

Understanding how to improve enforcement in a world of constrained resources is a significant challenge, but one of the hopeful aspects of regulation is that in recent years a new and vibrant scholarship has emerged. One aspect of this scholarship is a more sophisticated view of how regulators behave and how the recipients of regulation, firms, respond. These insights point to strategies for improving the effectiveness of regulation. In addition, worldwide concern about labor conditions in poor countries has driven a debate about how best to enforce standards under difficult circumstances. The situation is not exactly analogous to the American problem, since there is no international sovereign government with the capacity to impose sanctions, and therefore the debate is often about tactics to get around this constraint. But there is much to learn from the discussion.

We begin by asking about the standards that are currently on the books. We already saw in chapter 4 that some low-wage firms violate the law, and here we explore how to improve that situation. We then ask about new employment practices that create different challenges for regulation and propose possible new standards that would be appropriate. In the second part of this chapter, we consider local political movements aimed at creating new mechanisms for setting standards. These living wage and community benefits agreement campaigns are small-scale but have the potential to generate broad political support for more significant policies.

"Regulation" is a dirty word in much public discourse. It conjures up the image of heavy-handed government officials imposing unreasonable costs on employers. Certainly regulation can be done badly, and certainly we need to be thoughtful about the standards that are set and how they are enforced. The fact is that thoughtful regulations are effective in improving employment conditions. We saw earlier that the declining real value of the federal minimum wage is an important culprit in the rise of inequality, particularly in the 1980s, and we also saw that when the minimum wage is increased, the wage structure shifts up and wages tend to cluster around the new value. If regulation was inherently ineffective, neither of these patterns would occur. So regulation and standards can work, and in fact probably do work for the majority of employers who are law-abiding.

More generally, an all-encompassing rap against regulation is unfair. After all, it was deregulation of the financial sector that opened the door to the abusive behavior behind the collapse in 2008 and the subsequent economic crisis. A similar lesson follows from the BP oil spill in the Gulf of Mexico in 2010. These examples should be enough to make the simple point that regulation can be in the public interest. Regulations set the rules of the game, and in the labor market they can prevent firms from competing on the basis of squeezing labor. But labor market regulation is more than this. Americans have never been willing to view people as commodities, like pork bellies. We have always insisted on basic standards. Our regulatory structure is an expression of our values about what is fair and just, and we should not be ashamed to articulate these standards and search for the best ways to enforce them. We should also recognize that thoughtful regulation can create a virtuous circle: when faced with higher standards, employers want to improve productivity in order to meet the standards with minimal impact on their bottom line. Standards are an important component of any effort to improve the quality of low-wage work.

The Current State of Play: Inadequate Standards and Weak Enforcement

Modernizing regulations is important, but the impact of regulation depends as much on enforcement and compliance as it does on the content per se. In chapter 4, we showed that employment law violations in the low-wage labor market are discouragingly widespread. In the face of these violations, enforcement of employment standards is shockingly poor. The Obama administration, as one of its early actions, added about 250 inspectors to the Wage and Hour Division (WHD) of the Department of Labor, bringing the total to 900. Even so, over the past decades federal inspection resources have not kept pace with the growth of the workforce, and the probability of any firm being inspected is very low. Those inspectors must cover about 8 million workplaces.[1] Thus, for example, the probability that a fast-food restaurant affiliated with a national chain will be inspected in any given year is 0.008.[2] The current state of affairs reflects a long-term decline in resources.[3]

Additional inspection resources come from the states, but here too there is an overwhelming mismatch between the number of inspectors and the size of the workforce. The public interest organization Policy Matters Ohio surveyed states and found a total of 660 state inspectors in the forty-three states that responded.[4] These states accounted for about 90 percent of the national workforce. State inspectors often have broad responsibilities, and hence their attention to any particular issue—such as minimum wages or misclassification of occupations—is even more limited than the raw numbers suggest.[5] Some large states, such as Florida, have no inspectors enforcing minimum wages, while other states, even with larger staffs, have not kept up with population growth.[6]

The U.S. Government Accountability Office (GAO) documents the declining effectiveness of the Wage and Hour Division, the unit in the Department of Labor responsible for enforcement. In the GAO's words:

> Case studies show that WHD inadequately investigated complaints from low-wage and minimum wage workers alleging that employers failed to pay the federal minimum wage, required overtime, and failed to issue a last paycheck. . . . Examples of inadequate WHD responses to complaints included instances where WHD (1) inappropriately rejected complaints based on incorrect information provided by employers, (2) failed to make adequate attempts to locate employers, (3) did not thoroughly investigate and resolve complaints, and (4) delayed initiating investigations for over a year and then dropped the complaint because the statute of limitations for assessing back wages was close to expiring.[7]

Another GAO report went beyond case studies and examined the Department of Labor's database on wage and hour enforcement between 1997 and 2007.[8] It found that the number of enforcement actions dropped by one-third between those years and that the vast majority of those (72 percent) were in response to individual complaints rather than as part of a strategic effort to target firms or industries.

The bottom line is that enforcement resources are inadequate and what is available is poorly utilized. The other problem, however, is that within any reasonable budgetary expectation there will never be enough resources to meaningfully increase the probability that any given establishment will be inspected. So, beyond simply increasing resources, this raises the question: Can existing resources somehow be deployed so that their impact is amplified? And relatedly, are there alternative ways to think about enforcement that would enable us to move out of this box?

Adding to the challenge of compliance is that new employment practices add to the pressures on standards. This restructuring involves two of the behaviors that we described in chapter 4: changing ownership patterns (what David Weil calls the "fissuring" of employment) and increased use of outsourcing and subcontractors.[9] As we saw, these practices not only reduce wages but also increase the probability of violation of standards because the hiving out of some jobs into a more competitive sector of the job market creates strong pressures to squeeze labor costs and the decentralization of responsibility makes it less clear who is the real employer and thus who should bear responsibility for compliance. This creates opportunities for evasion, and it also complicates the work of regulators as they seek to affix responsibility.

These shifts create real challenges, but they are not new; indeed, ironically, they mark a return to past practice.[10] Garment industry job shops frequently used contractors to sew products, and these contractors were sometimes located on the job shop's premises and sometimes not. The job shops put enormous pressure on the contractors to minimize costs and were willing to shift work from one to another to drive prices—and wages—down. Violations of labor law were widespread. Similarly, farmers in California frequently used labor contractors to find workers for the harvest, and of course these people worked on the premises of the farm; the farmers refused to recognize them as employees, however, and not only turned a blind eye to any labor law violations but in fact encouraged violations in order to minimize costs. The practices of both garment industry job shops and California farming were the targets of reformers during the New Deal. While common sense might suggest that the top-level employer would bear some responsibility for standards violations, the law has not been successful in addressing the modern analogs of these practices.

Improving Enforcement

The foregoing forces us to think about how to improve enforcement. We organize this discussion into two parts: first we describe ideas and innovations that are possible within the current structure of regulation, and then we introduce some of the new thinking about regulation that has emerged in recent years.

STRATEGIC ENFORCEMENT

It is obvious that existing standards have been weakly enforced, and it certainly stands to reason that any new or revamped standards would face similar difficulties. Clearly it is important to address enforcement strategy directly, and it is also clear that any such discussion must begin by acknowledging a central defining fact: there will never be enough inspection resources to raise the probability of inspection faced by a random business to a level that is in any way a threat. The economy is simply too big, and resources will always be too limited, regardless of who holds political power.

It should also be understood that the success of various enforcement strategies is not independent of the nature of the standards that are set. For example, some standards can be more or less effectively enforced via data collection and record-keeping while others require on-site inspections. Nonetheless, it is helpful to begin by laying out the choices with respect to enforcement strategy. As Boston University scholar David Weil has made clear, a more strategic approach can have a noticeable impact on outcomes.[11]

Being strategic essentially means understanding industry structure and taking advantage of the points of leverage that such an understanding offers. In almost all variations of this approach, the key idea is that a large "mother" firm sits on top of a web of suppliers or franchisees. There may be employment law violations at the level of the mother firm, but it is more likely that the serious violations occur among the lower-level players. This pattern speaks directly to the discussion in chapter 4 about so many employers in low-wage labor market having organized themselves into webs of subcontractors. In this perspective on enforcement, pressure exerted on the top-level firm will be much more effective in obtaining compliance from its contractors than any direct pressure from the government. Examples of such opportunities are the garment industry, which has long been based on a network of subcontractors; hotels, which outsource services such as food preparation and laundry; national fast-food brands, whose reputation depends on the performance of franchisees; and large retail firms such as Wal-Mart, which exert considerable power over their suppliers.

There have been a number of successes from pursuing this strategy. In the garment industry, an enforcement campaign used the "hot goods" provision of the Fair Labor Standards Act, which permits the government to block shipment to firms of goods produced by suppliers that are found in violation of employment law.[12] This threat has teeth because of the widespread adoption of low-inventory rapid-order fulfillment systems, which impose substantial costs on suppliers and retailers when delays are encountered. With this threat, the Labor Department has also been able to force brand-goods firms to pressure their suppliers to improve compliance. Other examples along these lines include a targeted enforcement action in the fast-food industry that led national brands to pressure franchises to improve compliance.[13]

BRINGING IN NEW PLAYERS

In an environment of constrained resources, enforcement agencies can use all the help they can get. In many communities whose members work in low-wage sectors, an impressive array of community and advocacy groups has emerged to help improve conditions. Finding a way to cooperate with these groups can bring important advantages.

An example of what can be accomplished with this strategy is New York State's efforts to involve community groups—such as immigrants' rights organizations, workers' centers, social service agencies, and unions—in enforcement practice. The Enforcement Division of the State Department of Labor created a department of senior-level staffers whose exclusive job is working with these community organizations. Several benefits flow from this cooperation. One is that these organizations have deep contacts in their communities and hence access to people and information that is unavailable to government agencies. For example, such organizations can effectively reassure workers that the Enforcement Division is not in cahoots with immigration authorities and hence that coming forward with complaints is not risky.

The second benefit is more subtle but probably more important. The community groups can help the enforcement staff understand the industry and the nature of violations more thoroughly than they could on their own. A good example from New York State is the racetrack industry. Racetracks employ large numbers of low-wage workers who take care of horses and do various cleaning jobs. The problem is that they work very odd hours, and wage and hours enforcers have a hard time knowing when to show up. Furthermore, the pay system is unusual: often workers are paid per horse rather than per hour. After gaining the trust of an immigrants' rights organization, the state Wage and Hours Division was able to work with its staff to figure out the scheduling at the tracks and the relationships between the pay systems and the hours worked, and this in turn led to effective enforcement actions. This kind of deep knowledge can be obtained only through the kinds of relationships that this New York State agency has cultivated.

It is important to understand that in this example the state did not "deputize" or otherwise give the advocacy groups any official standing. Although there have been proposals along these lines, this strategy can quickly run into civil service opposition and a range of liability problems. Short of this step, however, it is clear that working with advocacy groups provides significant advantages.

THE SMALL-BUSINESS CONUNDRUM

We have seen that about one-third of low-wage workers are employed in small businesses, and there is every reason to believe that employment law violations are at least as problematic in these employers as in large firms. The reason is not that small-business owners are more rapacious than their counterparts in large firms, but rather that they are under intense pressure and also lack the managerial capacity—a dedicated human resources department, for example—to keep track of requirements and compliance. This rationale, combined with the considerable political power of the small-business lobby, has resulted in very small firms being exempted from a range of regulatory requirements. However, given the importance of small employers in the low-wage labor market, and given the intense pressures on these employers to squeeze out profit margins, it is important to think realistically about whether regulation of this sector can be effective.

The first step is to get past the view that small firms are inherently antigovernment. This perception flows in large part from the political lobbying of the National Federation of Independent Businesses (NFIB), which is widely regarded as one of the most powerful lobbies in Washington. NFIB claims to speak for small businesses and consistently takes hostile positions on issues such as increases in the minimum wage and health care reform. However, there is reason to believe that a great many small-business owners are more open to constructive public policy than is suggested by the positions of the

NFIB. In an American Express poll conducted in 2000, 82 percent of small-business owners cited "improving schools/training of young people for work" as a very important issue for them, and a 2007 poll found, perhaps surprisingly, that a significant majority of small-business owners were supportive of a minimum wage increase.[14]

Additional evidence on this point comes from polling conducted after passage of the Massachusetts health care insurance legislation, a reform that prefigured to a great degree the national health care reform measures passed in 2010. In response to the question "Do you agree that health care reform has been good for Massachusetts?" 50 percent of employers in firms of three to ten workers responded affirmatively, as did 53 percent of employers of eleven to fifty workers. In firms of one thousand or more employees, the figure was 59 percent. Hence, the gap between large and small businesses was nowhere near as large as is often portrayed.[15] In response to the proposition "All employers bear some responsibility for providing health benefits to their workers," 74 percent of the smallest firms responded positively, as did 79 percent of employers with eleven to fifty employees.[16]

If small firms are not the implacable enemies of government they are sometimes portrayed to be, there is still a question of whether policy can effectively reach them given the inherent difficulty posed by large numbers of small enterprises. In fact, it is certainly the case that the majority of small firms want to obey the law and that hence, if they are aware of employment regulations, those regulations will have an impact. In addition, experience in other regulatory realms suggests optimistic conclusions. A particularly compelling example is a recent detailed case study of regulatory enforcement of environmental rules in the dry cleaning industry.[17]

Dry cleaning is dominated by small firms, and in both California and Massachusetts the majority are Korean. Both states implemented similar chemical regulations in the late 1990s. In Massachusetts, compliance rates skyrocketed from 10 percent when the regulations were implemented to well over 80 percent a few years later, whereas in California compliance remained low. The research underlying the case was aimed at understanding why this difference emerged, and the answer pointed directly to different regulatory strategies and the key role played by the Massachusetts employers' association.

In Massachusetts, in contrast to California, the regulatory authority worked cooperatively with the Korean dry cleaners' business association to develop rules and compliance procedures. After fifteen months of conversation and negotiations, the two sides agreed on a set of straightforward compliance questions and a simple workbook. In addition, extensive interviewing demonstrated that the regulators' relationships with the firms were based on trust, not on "gotcha"-style inspections and penalties. The consequence was that within the Massachusetts community of dry cleaners strong norms emerged that encouraged compliance because it came to be seen as the right thing to do. In addition, the employers' association itself provided technical assistance and, in meetings, advocated for the importance of compliance for both individual firms and the group as a whole. The state inspectors also helped with technical assistance on both machines and record-keeping. Their attitude was that in small businesses problems with compliance are often inadvertent.

Some features of the dry cleaners case in Massachusetts are unique, particularly the strong desire of a minority Korean community for social acceptance, a motivation that was not present among the much more numerous Koreans in California. Nonetheless, two important lessons emerge from this case: the importance of regulatory authorities taking a collaborative attitude, and the role of business associations in diffusing information and establishing norms. Although norms are not formally binding, a very long tradition of social science research points to their power. When firms are members of an association through which they interact with other enterprises, there is every reason to believe that normative influence will be important. And fortunately, many small firms are members of industry associations.

Rethinking Regulation

In recent years, scholars have engaged in a serious rethinking of regulatory strategies, motivated in part by a long-standing political science literature that recognizes the need to understand enforcement in a context broader than a simple focus on budgetary issues (for example, the number of inspectors) and to take into account the inherently uneven and uncertain nature of implementation. A second major impetus has been the impact of globalization and growing interest in finding ways to manage its deleterious impact on working conditions in poorer nations. This latter concern has contributed to the rethinking of regulatory strategies because, on the one hand, governments in poor nations often have limited capacity and, on the other hand, at an international level there is no sovereign entity with enforcement power.

These two strands of thinking—the focus on the realities of execution and the search for strategies in a world of uneven governmental authority—sometimes operate on separate tracks and sometimes come together. It might seem that at first glance both have more to do with the design of enforcement mechanisms than with what the actual standards should be, but this would be a misreading of the discussion. The standards that are set affect the enforcement process, and so at least some discussions of improving regulation focus on both sides of the equation.

The more realistic view of implementation flows from an understanding that regulators are what has been termed "street-level bureaucrats" who operate in a world of inherently limited resources: "The decisions of street-level bureaucrats, the routines they establish, and the devices they invent to cope with uncertainties and work pressures effectively become the public policies they carry out."[18] The challenge for enforcers, who never have enough resources to carry out the letter of the law, lies in exercising discretion and making choices.

The second element of realism is based on an understanding of the behavior of the firm or organization on the receiving end of regulation. In a series of case studies, Susan Silbey and her colleagues distinguished between situations where the firm sees the regulator as a threat, as an ally, or simply as an obstacle to be overcome.[19] Depending on these interpretations, firms comply with the regulations, seek to fool the regulator (for example, by cleaning up their operations during visits and subsequently returning to business as usual), or simply devise work-arounds that enable them to do whatever they want to do. Whether the regulator is ultimately successful in achieving his or her goals turns out to depend in important measure on how the firm views the process.

Globalization introduces a different set of ideas into the regulation discussion: how to generate pressures for better behavior when there is no international law and, assuming this is possible, how to monitor and enforce compliance in a world of weak or absent governments. Adding to the difficulties is the emerging structure of the international production system: the use of extensive supply chains involving subcontractors and, frequently, second- or even third-level subcontractors. This deeply complicates not only the question of assigning responsibility but also issues of monitoring and compliance.

New Models of Regulation

One set of ideas makes a virtue of necessity and advocates a system that is explicitly based on the discretion of the enforcement bureaucracy. This emerges from observing what Michael Piore and Andrew Schrank term the "Latin model" of regulation because it characterizes the practice in France, Spain, and much of Latin America.[20] In the current American system, there are separate statutes and separate enforcement bureaucracies for each of our many regulations: wage and hours, health and safety, equal employment opportunity, and so on. By contrast, in the Latin model these are all combined in a labor law code and enforced by one agency. The advantages are that the labor inspector can observe the full range of issues in a firm and make trade-offs between problems that urgently need fixing and those that can wait. In addition, the spirit of these inspections is, in the words of observers, "compliance," not "sanctions"—the inspector is oriented toward helping the firm improve rather than punishing it. Of course, possible sanctions are always in the background, but the main role of the inspector is to achieve progress. Because the inspectors work with a range of firms in an industry and geographic area, they can often act as expert consultants in helping the firm improve its practices. An extension of the model gives inspectors access to resources to assist firms in training their workforces, obtaining financing, and upgrading technology.

Other strategies for improving regulation derive from efforts to improve standards in international supply chains. The elements of a solution are consumer-driven pressures for improvement, voluntary standards, independent as well as mother firm–based monitors, and disclosure of information. These elements have been combined by different researchers and advocates in varying mixes, but the solutions tend to be more similar than not. Most generically, consumers insist that the products they buy be manufactured under decent conditions, and so the final-stage or branding firm issues a set of standards for its subcontractors. These standards are made public so that consumers can monitor them. The final-stage firm has its own internal compliance inspection system but also contracts with an independent monitoring agency (a number of which have emerged). The results of the monitoring are made public on a regular basis so that pressure for improvement is maintained. The hope is not only that this process will lead to improvements in the supply chain of the final-stage firm, but also that it will diffuse to the firm's competitors in a "racheting-up" process as they seek to emulate and keep pace in the market.[21] Other ideas touch on the ways in which the mother firm can work with its suppliers to improve their practice rather than simply acting as an enforcement and punishment mechanism.[22]

The analogy between the United States and the problems of international standards is not exact because in this country there is a central government with considerable power. Nonetheless, the international model could lead to some potentially promising innovations in the U.S. context. As we have seen, there has been a growing use of subcontractors and outsourcing in the U.S. labor market, and this raises issues analogous to the problems posed by international supply chains. In addition, at least some American firms have shown an interest in developing their own standards and monitoring their own behavior.

All of these ideas—whether those derived from the Latin model or those inspired by the experience of global labor standards—are attractive. They acknowledge the realities of enforcement on the ground and the need to move regulation whenever possible to a win-win model rather than one based purely on sanctions. They also recognize that at least some employers can be motivated to improve their practices, in which case these employers are likely to be much more successful if given greater freedom of action (combined with a sharp eye on their activities by their workforces or external monitors). Improving regulatory strategies is therefore an area with fertile opportunities for experimentation by both federal and state authorities.

This being said, there is also reason for caution. One concern is that to reduce the regulatory burden on firms, and hence to limit political opposition, predictability is important, yet the core of the Latin model is the individual discretion of enforcers. Second, the Latin model as an overarching strategy does not appear to be realistic in the U.S. context because it would require a wholesale rewriting of a panoply of employment laws as well as a massive bureaucratic reorganization. Nevertheless, there is something to be learned regarding the advantages of coordination across multiple agencies that are responsible for regulating employment practices. Effective coordination would multiply enforcement resources and would also at least open the possibility of easing the regulatory burden on firms while at the same time improving outcomes. An example of a step in this direction can be found in New York State, which has pushed collaboration among the Enforcement Division, the Unemployment Insurance Division, the Workers' Compensation Division, and the Division of Tax and Finance. Inspectors from one division now inform the others of any violations they spot, and more important, there has been cross-training so that each division's inspectors are educated regarding the issues and procedures of the others. This kind of coordination enables much more effective and comprehensive compliance actions than in the past.

Beyond Regulation As We Know It

Employment standards are the traditional way in which government has sought to shape working conditions and to set minimum standards. In recent years, however, new strategies have emerged, notably community benefits agreements (CBAs) and living wage campaigns. Two aspects of these efforts are notable. First, the arena in which they are implemented—most typically cities and sometimes even neighborhoods of cities—is local. Second, these strategies are usually fought for by grassroots community organizations that are sometimes linked to labor unions but often are not. As such, community benefits agreements and living wage ordinances represent an important and potentially powerful mixture of strategies. They can raise standards in their own right by virtue of the provisions in the law or agreement, but perhaps more importantly, they are a vehicle that enables people to organize and mobilize around their concerns for economic fairness. To the extent that this happens, the specific legislative or negotiated achievements may be less important than the subsequent shift in the political balance of power.

COMMUNITY BENEFITS AGREEMENTS

The local government approval required for any large-scale construction or development project provides a potential source of leverage that can be employed to push up work standards.[23] Consider, as an example, the construction of a shopping mall. The project will obviously create work, and an important question is, who will get those jobs? What fraction of jobs, if any, will be set aside for residents of nearby low-income communities, and what kind of training will be provided that might enable future access to high-quality construction work? After the mall is completed there will be many retail jobs, and we have already seen that retail jobs typically pay too little and provide few opportunities for upward mobility. The future owners of the mall might be induced to promise higher wages in return for zoning approval.

This scenario adds up to what have been termed community benefits agreements, which are efforts by advocacy groups to leverage the zoning power of local government to obtain improvements in job quality. CBAs received national attention in 2001 when developers of the Staples Center in Los Angeles signed an agreement with the city and a coalition of community groups.

A sense of the process involved in obtaining a CBA can be gained by looking at a 2006 CBA covering the development of the Yale–New Haven Hospital (YNHH) Cancer Center, the primary teaching hospital for the Yale University Medical School. When Yale announced in 2004 its intention to build a cancer center, Community Organized for Responsible Development (CORD) began to mobilize around this project. CORD initially consisted of twenty-two community, labor, and faith-based organizations.[24] The organization employed five organizers and utilized numerous volunteers to go door to door to over eight hundred homes in the community adjacent to the hospital, documenting community concerns. CORD began to develop a list of community goals for the CBA and held biweekly meetings of its members to maintain momentum and facilitate communication during the two-year campaign.[25]

CORD was ultimately able to prevail in part because it mobilized large numbers of residents and maintained strong connections with political allies. For example, CORD sent two hundred members to a September 2004 public meeting held by the hospital to present a proposed parking project. In May 2005, CORD conducted a rally with several thousand participants during Yale's graduation week. On the political side, CORD succeeded in getting the New Haven Board of Aldermen to pass a resolution in the summer of 2004 that encouraged developers to negotiate CBAs and mentioned CBAs as a potential factor in project approval.[26] Ultimately, both the mayor of New Haven and the Board of Aldermen indicated that they would withhold needed permits for the project until a CBA was negotiated. In March 2006, Yale agreed to sign the CBA.

The final CBA included provisions for $1.2 million in affordable housing and economic development, a commitment to hire five hundred neighborhood residents over five years, a job ladder program with fifty spaces, a local hiring target for women and minorities for construction jobs, improved access

Figure 5.1   CBA Deal Status, 2011

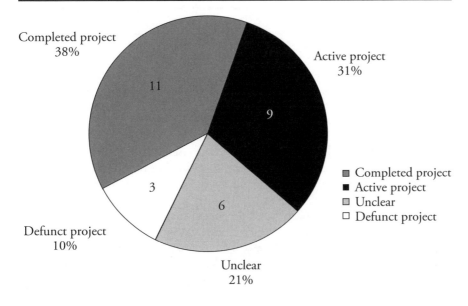

Source: Authors' calculations. See chapter 5, note 27, for further details on data sources.
Note: Numbers in pie slices represent number of CBAs.

to free care for poor residents, and a variety of other items relating to youth, traffic, and environmental issues. In addition, the CBA contained language giving employees the right to organize a union in a neutral environment.

The Extent and Impact of CBAs

How widespread are CBAs, and what is their impact? To answer this question, we reviewed the literature and tallied up all CBAs that could be identified. Figure 5.1 shows the number of CBAs across the nation, and table 5.1 provides an upper and lower bound of our estimates regarding the number of jobs that are affected. (See note 27 for our methodology for arriving at these estimates.)[27]

These data suggest that the overall impact of CBAs, even if we accept the upper-bound estimates, is quite modest. In addition, the impact is probably further diminished when it comes to actual implementation, as opposed to estimates derived from plans. For example, accounts of the New Haven agreement suggest that the hospital has not followed through on its hiring

Table 5.1   Lower and Upper Bounds of Jobs Affected by CBAs, 2011

	Lower Bound	Upper Bound
Construction jobs	16,672	137,108
Permanent jobs	34,841	118,074
Total	51,513	255,182

Source: Authors' calculations. See chapter 5, note 27, for further details on data sources.

agreement.[28] A recent overall review of CBAs concluded: "Because CBAs are a relatively recent phenomenon, there is insufficient evidence to evaluate whether they provide a net benefit either to parties to the agreement or to others."[29]

Given this modest impact, what are we to make of CBAs? We return to this question after we discuss living wage campaigns, but for now we would say that it is most useful to think of CBAs as devices around which the broader debate about job quality can be organized. Thought of in these terms, the impact of CBAs may be substantially greater than the figures reported here imply.

Contracting and Living Wages

Federal, state, and local governments contract for an enormous range of services, and many of these jobs are of low quality. This practice does, however, offer an opportunity to use government purchasing leverage to raise the floor in the job market. One strategy is to establish and enforce more effectively federal standards for contracts. In addition, a great deal of creative energy has been expended at the local level, particularly on living wage ordinances.

As government agencies outsource more of their functions to private contractors, the issue of job quality in these contractors becomes more salient. At the federal level, spending on contract goods and services rose 69 percent from 2000 to 2006. During this same time period, the number of federal contract workers rose from 1.4 million to 2 million. Contract workers now make up 43 percent of the workforce that is producing goods and services for the government.[30] A recent analysis of contracting data reported that 20 percent of federal contract employees earned less than the poverty level for a family of four, as opposed to 8 percent of direct federal workers.[31] Furthermore, contracting in low-wage service industries, such as janitorial services and food preparation, has grown more rapidly than it has in higher-wage industries. In addition to highlighting low contractor wages, researchers also have noted that many federal contractors have poor records with regard to labor, health, safety, and tax laws.[32]

Advocates, particularly the National Employment Law Project and the Center for American Progress, have described in considerable detail the steps the federal government could take to improve job quality within contractors.[33] These include improved enforcement of legislation already on the books, such as the Service Contract Act, as well as new measures such as prioritizing contractors who offer high-quality jobs.

In states and communities, the best-known policy for improving the terms of employment for government contractors is a living wage law—local legislation that raises wages for a targeted group of employees who work for firms that in some way do business with a city. The first living wage ordinance was passed in Baltimore in 1994 as a result of organizing by a community group affiliated with the national Industrial Areas Foundation network, and since then, the best estimate is that about 140 such ordinances have been implemented throughout the country. This is certainly an underestimate because a number of living wage campaigns do not aim to pass laws but rather press public authorities to raise the wages of employees and contractors through administrative methods. Unlike community benefits agreements, which tend to be concentrated on the coasts, particularly the West Coast, living wage ordinances are relatively evenly spread across the nation's four regions.[34] Some are aimed at contractors working on city contracts, others at anyone doing business with the city, some at firms receiving business assistance such as tax breaks, and yet others at city employees.

There is an emerging evaluation literature on living wage campaigns. What is striking is that even skeptics concede that the ordinances are successful in raising wages. The debate is over whether there are negative employment effects, but again, even the skeptics accept that, if there is any impact on employment, the wage gains outweigh the costs and as a result there is a net benefit to low-wage employees and their families; in fact, the bulk of the literature finds no negative employment consequences.[35] Studies of the impact on firms do not find major negative effects, and some suggest that turnover is reduced as a result of the higher wages.[36]

We have already seen that the number of people affected by community benefits agreements is very small when put in a national context. Much the same can be said about living wage campaigns, since most such campaigns affect only several hundred workers and even the largest affect a very small fraction of a city's workforce.[37] What, then, are we to make of these efforts? In our view, these campaigns and subsequent agreements are best viewed as political tools that help advocates organize around economic equity and, if successful, put equity issues on the local political agenda. The evidence on this point is scattered but nonetheless plausible. For example, the widespread success of the ballot initiatives to raise state minimum wages (described in chapter 1) can at least in part be attributed to groundwork laid in many of these states by prior living wage campaigns.

An extension of the living wage idea is to attach standards to the very substantial economic development subsidies—tax breaks and direct incentives—that localities and states frequently use to attract firms to their area. These subsidies, which are used for everything from sports stadiums to call centers, are controversial because it is often not clear that the benefits of job creation outweigh the costs of lost tax revenue. Despite this concern, local officials feel whipsawed into offering these goodies because, without them, firms threaten to locate elsewhere. This is not the place to enter into this debate, but it is important to note that localities are now more often requiring that firms pay living wages to their employees. An example of such an ordinance is in Philadelphia:

> The ordinance applies to city contractors with contracts worth more than $10,000 and recipients of city financial aid in excess of $100,000, as well as lessees of city property. It sets the living wage at 150 percent of the federal minimum wage. It includes a clause on health benefits, which states that an employer must provide health insurance if it provides benefits to some full-time employees elsewhere in the firm. The ordinances mandate a living wage advisory commission to oversee enforcement, of which businesses may represent no more than 4/9 of the members.[38]

In many respects, these laws are more important than the more standard living wage contractor ordinances, because incentives of this kind are so widespread. Furthermore, they are attractive vehicles for organizing around economic fairness because it is possible to appeal to a broader taxpayer base. For example, pressuring economic development authorities to insist on living wages has been the centerpiece of Industrial Area Foundation organizing campaigns in San Antonio, the Rio Grande Valley, and Austin. Again, however, the question is whether these requirements cost jobs, and again, as in the minimum wage debate, the answer is no. The best available evaluation of these laws and requirements used longitudinal data on firms over nearly a twenty-year period and matched cities that had passed laws with a comparable control group that had not.[39] The study found that that living wage requirements attached to economic development subsidies had no negative effect on employment growth in the cities as a whole, nor was there a downside for the specific industries most affected by the law. Just as was true for minimum wages, the critiques based on standard theory are wrong: it is indeed possible to push for better wages without adverse consequences.

Conclusion

Labor standards are a key tool for improving the low-wage labor market. They can set a floor, and they can also play a key role in prodding firms to improve by providing the "beneficial constraints" discussed earlier. The challenges of standards are threefold. First, enforcement and compliance must be improved. Second, the level of existing standards—for example, the minimum wage—need to be raised. Third, enforcement strategies need to be reconsidered in light of the inherent scarcity of resources. Happily, there has been a great deal of both thinking and experimentation on all of these dimensions. In addition, new strategies, particularly living wage campaigns, have succeeded as organizing tools in mobilizing political support for steps to improve job quality.

Having said this, it must also be acknowledged that the specter of stronger and more extensive employment standards is likely to kindle considerable controversy. It would certainly be sensible to think carefully about how to make labor standards more palatable to firms and therefore to public opinion. The first step is to observe that, in fact, there is broader support for employment standards than is often apparent in antigovernment rhetoric. Recall the consistent polling result that the public overwhelmingly approves of minimum wage increases, and recall that when people all around the nation enter the voting booth, they have supported these increases. Recall also that small businesses are not nearly as opposed to sensible regulation as some Washington lobbying groups would have us believe. All this is true, but we can still find ways to improve standards enforcement.

Effective regulation and employment standards should be predictable and should not be burdensome to firms that have a strong track record of compliance. A proposal for identifying and rewarding firms that have demonstrated a commitment to compliance has been put forward by NYU Law School professor Cynthia Estlund, using the label "co-regulation."[40] The core idea of co-regulation is that under some circumstances firms, particularly brand-conscious firms with supply chains, will bend to consumer pressure and upgrade their labor conditions. A classic example is the success of an organization of Florida tomato pickers, operating under the threat of a consumer boycott, in convincing Taco Bell and Burger King to insist that the labor contractors who hired the pickers improve their wages and working conditions. Estlund proposes to extend this model and to grant firms that agree to improve their practices a degree of flexibility with respect to standard employment law enforcement. This is broadly consistent with modern ideas about good management in which a central authority sets goals but leaves it to those more directly responsible to decide how best to achieve them. An independent monitor is needed to make this system reliable, and the natural actor here is employee voice—a union or other form of employee organization—within the enterprise. Hence the term "co-regulation."

Co-regulation entails its own set of challenges. One is the obvious one—that we are a long way from a world in which there is adequate employee representation to play the role of the "co" in co-regulation. Without this balance, the idea might be open to considerable slippage. The other problem is that the best examples of co-regulation in action, or even in theory, center on the behavior of large, sophisticated firms with the capacity to develop standards and monitor them. However, the employer landscape in the low-wage labor market is much more variegated, and any regulatory strategy must take this into account. All this being said, the core idea of rewarding employers that are in compliance and focusing enforcement resources where the real problem lies is both sensible when viewed through an enforcement lens and attractive in that it promises to make employment standards less politically controversial and more acceptable to the broader employer community.

In the best of cases, the enforcement of standards can be combined with assistance to firms to help them meet expectations. But even when enforcement is not tightly linked to upgrading, the hope is that firms will still be responsive to other efforts to assist them, given that they have to comply with the legal and political pressure to improve job quality. The brutal competitive conditions that many employers confront today give them an additional incentive for upgrading. In chapter 8, we discuss how to assist firms, but first we turn to another source of pressure for improvement: employee voice.

CHAPTER 6

Voice and Power

Las Vegas holds a special place in the American imagination. What started off as a mission founded in 1855 by thirty Mormons then became a haven for the Mafia and, by the twenty-first century, transformed itself into an embodiment of several versions of the American dream. For some, Vegas is the place where their luck will turn and they will make their fortune at the tables. But for many others, Vegas is a jobs machine, the city where they will find work and build a decent life. Until the financial crisis, Vegas was the fastest-growing city in America. People came for work and they found it.

What is badly paid work in many parts of the country is well paid in Vegas. For instance, a nonmanagerial food service worker in Las Vegas earns $10.50 an hour compared to $8.25 an hour in Orlando, Florida, which is a fair comparison in terms of industry distribution, demographics, and cost of living. A hotel room cleaner in Vegas averages $12 an hour versus $8 an hour in Orlando.[1]

An important part of the Las Vegas jobs story lies in the role of unions. Underlying the relatively high wages that moderately educated employees earn in Las Vegas, and the related fact that jobs that are poorly paid and lacking in benefits in many parts of the country are good jobs in Vegas, is the power of the local unions. An understanding of unions in Vegas must begin with local 226 of the Hotel Employees and Restaurant Employees Union (HERE), a local universally known as the Culinary Workers Union. This union plays a central role in raising wages for many of the employees—maids, busboys, line cooks—who make the Strip into a money machine.

The Culinary Workers did not always have the power to play this role. For many years it was a mob-controlled local dominated by Elmer "Al" Bramlet, a colorful figure who delivered for his members but also for the mob. He dominated the local from 1954 until 1977, when he was murdered, allegedly by mobster Tony "The Ant" Spilotro, the enforcer who was the inspiration for the Joe Pesci character in Martin Scorsese's movie *Casino*. In 1995, the Justice Department took control of HERE. Eventually the national union reorganized the local, putting into place a leadership that was committed to giving its members a strong voice in decisions and governance. Today, a visit to the local reveals a vibrant political culture that would put many unions across the country to shame.

This power did not come easily. A sixty-seven-day strike in 1984 ended with the decertification of the union in six hotels. The union gradually regained its footing as key corporate-owned casinos, such as Circus Circus and the Mirage, negotiated contracts. But in 1991 the Frontier cut wages and benefits and unilaterally changed work rules. This represented a potential change in the pattern that the union could not accept. The resulting strike lasted six bitter years, but had a happier outcome when the casino eventually settled. The victory in this strike, in which most of the Las Vegas establishment sided with the union, remains a major theme in the local 226 culture. Today the vast majority of corporate-owned Strip hotels recognize that their relationship with the union is mutually beneficial.

In addition to bargaining over wages, the union has also created one of the best-known training and career ladder programs in the nation. Its contract with the Strip hotels funds a large union-run training center and commits the hotels to using it as a hiring source for good middle-level jobs in kitchens and in customer-facing functions. We interviewed employers, trainers, and workers at this training center just as the recession was beginning to bite hard and hiring had slowed down considerably. Nonetheless, it was clear that the training center was successful in opening mobility pathways for employees. At the time of our visit, the center was training about three thousand employees per year in a wide range of skills. Our interviews with employees provided numerous examples of upward mobility.

It is important not to romanticize Las Vegas. The unions have not been successful in organizing many of the off-Strip hotels, and overall the percentage of employees who are paid below our standard is nearly as high in Vegas as it is in Orlando. Furthermore, as is well known, the financial crisis that hit in the fall of 2008 brought the good times in Las Vegas to an end. Since then, housing prices have plummeted, unemployment is high, and large-scale construction projects have gone bankrupt. However, these facts do not obviate the main point: employees who work in classically low-wage, no-future jobs in Strip hotels have had their lives radically improved by the union.

It is reasonable to worry that Las Vegas is a special case because of the tremendous resources of the Strip hotels and also because of the historical relationship between the mob, the unions, and the employers, which some may believe (although they say so sotto voce) influenced the bargaining. But Las

Vegas is not the only example of successful organizing among low-wage workers. Consider the well-known case of Justice for Janitors, an organizing campaign of the Service Workers International Union (SEIU). Justice for Janitors (JfJ) obtains union contracts for the people who clean commercial buildings, classic low-wage work whose workers and extensive subcontracting represent much of what is happening in the low-wage job market. Although JfJ has organized campaigns in at least thirty cities, the best-known and most successful example is in Los Angeles.

SEIU started as a union representing building cleaners. The union dramatically lost ground in Los Angeles when building owners began to outsource the work to cleaning firms, and those firms in turn hired large numbers of immigrants, often undocumented. The immigrant share of the cleaning workforce grew from 28 percent in 1980 to 61 percent in 1990.[2] Meanwhile, the fraction of the downtown market organized by SEIU fell from 33 percent in 1977 to 8 percent in 1985.[3] It appeared that the jobs were on an inevitable downhill slide.

Faced with this challenge, the union innovated in several important ways. In addition to aiming at the cleaning companies themselves, the union targeted building owners and did so via marches and publicity, tactics that are legal under the National Labor Relations Act. These political actions drew heavily on a mobilized Latino community, and the union-organizing campaign took on the idiom and aura of the civil rights movement. Put differently, the union became a social movement and connected to the community in ways that unions had historically done but that had seemingly been long lost. In addition, the union innovated a number of clever tactics, such as trigger agreements, under which cleaning companies agreed to accept the union provided that a given number of their competitors did. This tactic reduced opposition stemming from the fear that acceptance of the union would lead a firm to be undercut by lower-wage, non-union competitors. Following a difficult organizing campaign, one marked by a violent police attack on marchers in Century City, which in turn was followed by an outpouring of political and church support, the union succeeded in organizing and substantially raising the wages of the low-wage building cleaners in Los Angeles.

The Los Angeles story shows what is possible, but it would be naive to ignore aspects of the campaign that raise questions about the general lessons that can be drawn or the complexities that need to be considered concerning union tactics. We return to these questions later, but for now it is clear from both the Las Vegas and L.A. stories that employee voice can have a powerful impact on improving conditions for low-wage workers. We also shortly see that, in addition to unions, a wide range of community organizations have worked to improve job quality through campaigns organized around living wages, worker centers, and numerous other initiatives. The best hope for

Figure 6.1   Wages and Unionization Among Employees with a High School
Degree or Less, by Occupation, 2007 to 2010

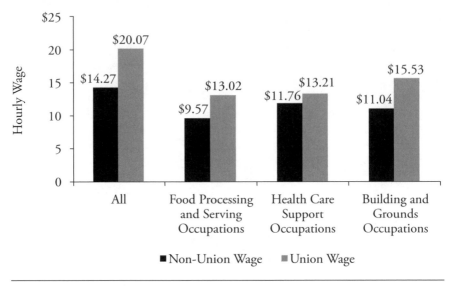

Source: Authors' calculations. See chapter 1 appendix for further details on data sources.
Note: Data for 2007 to 2009 are combined to obtain larger samples sizes.

strengthening employee voice is a more effective coalition between these groups and traditional unions.

What the Data Tell Us

Data on union membership and wages make it clear: the benefits that unions bring to low-wage workers are indisputable. One simple way to see this is to compare the wages of employees who are unionized with the wages of those who are not. Figure 6.1 provides these data for employees with a high school degree or less, and figure 6.2 does the same for those with some college. The first pair of bars of each figure includes all employees, and the other pairs further limit the sample to employees in quintessential low-wage occupations.

Relatively poorly educated employees in low-wage occupations are much better off if their wages are negotiated by unions. This is true across the board, and the gains are substantial. For example, high school–educated workers who clean buildings gain $4 an hour, a very large boost. The benefit is smaller for health care support workers (the technicians and orderlies who work in health facilities), but even for them the improvement is $2 an hour.

How do these estimates vary for men and women and for different ethnic

Figure 6.2   Wages and Unionization Among Employees with Some College, by Occupation, 2007 to 2010

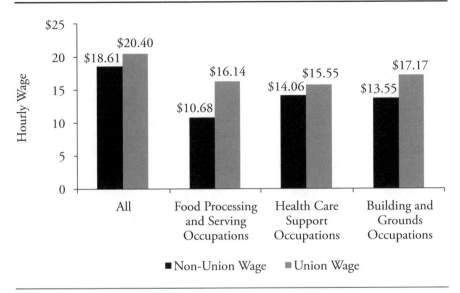

Source: Authors' calculations. See chapter 1 appendix for further details on data sources.
Note: Data for 2007 to 2009 are combined to obtain larger samples sizes.

and racial groups? Table 6.1 answers this question by showing the percentage wage gain from unionization that obtains after controlling in a statistical model for occupation and age as well as gender and race or ethnicity. Again, the benefits of unionization for low-wage workers are very substantial.

The benefits of unionization extend beyond wages. Unions often negotiate agreements that substantially boost the amount of training provided to low-wage workers and create pathways for them to move into better jobs. Prominent examples can be found in health care, where unions in New York and Philadelphia have established very large training programs. Another well-known example is in the hospitality industry in Las Vegas.

VOICE OUTSIDE THE WORKPLACE

There are no data in the census surveys on community organizations; however, fieldwork and observation provide convincing testimony of their impact. Indeed, over the past several decades there has been, somewhat under the radar screen, a flowering of these groups, and the number of organizations and their broad geographical dispersion may well be a surprise to those who believe that the energy behind progressive reform has abated. Commu-

Table 6.1   Union Premium for People with a High School Degree or Less, 2007 to 2010

	All Occupations	Food Processing and Serving Occupations	Health Care Support Occupations	Buildings and Grounds Occupations
Men	+34%	+25%	+29%	+29%
Women	+20	+26	+13	+31
Blacks	+19	+19	+23	+28
Hispanics	+20	+20	—	+33
Whites	+24	+24	+10	+34

Source: Authors' calculations. See chapter 1 appendix for further details on data sources.

Notes: These are coefficients from a regression of ln(wages) on union status and age. Each cell is the result of a regression with the sample limited to the group identified in the cell as well as being limited to people with a high school degree or less. For example, the +25 percent in the cell labeled "men, food processing and serving" means that in a regression of men with a high school degree or less whose occupation was food processing or serving, the union coefficient in the regression in which the dependent variable was the logarithm of wage and that also included age was 0.25. The sample size was too small to provide an estimate for Hispanics in health care.

nity organizations, worker centers, and interfaith groups are active in virtually all large metropolitan areas and have chalked up numerous victories, ranging from local living wage campaigns to statewide minimum wage reform to funds for expanded job training programs. The problem, of course, is one of scale, in light of the enormous size of the American labor market. But before we address this concern, it is important to understand the real possibilities that these organizations offer.

Perhaps the best national example of these organizations is the network of industrial areas foundation (IAF) organizations, which are successors of the pioneering work of Saul Alinsky, the man who virtually invented community organizing in America.[4] Alinsky, a graduate of the University of Chicago Sociology Department, began organizing during the 1930s. Closely associated with the union-organizing drives that were exploding during this era, as well as with the Catholic hierarchy in Chicago, Alinsky created a style of organizing that proved remarkably durable. President Obama was trained in IAF organizing techniques during his stint as an organizer in Chicago.

Organizing along IAF lines has already attained impressive dimensions. A recent survey examined the diffusion of what the researchers termed "faith-based organizing" and identified 133 organizations in thirty-three states that in total have reached somewhere between one and three million people.[5] To give a sense of the magnitude of IAF organizing, in the Lower Rio Grande

Valley in Texas, the IAF organization Valley Interfaith has forty-five churches and sixteen schools as members, and these represent over 60,000 people. The IAF organization in Chicago, United Power for Action and Justice, has 300 member institutions. In Los Angeles, LA Metro is building toward a goal of 150 member congregations, ten member unions, and fifty member schools.

What does an IAF organization do? First on its list of priorities is leadership development and training. This is at the core of how the IAF defines its mission. Leaders are developed through one-on-one conversations, frequent training sessions, and conferences on issues in which the leaders take a prominent role in framing the discussion. Leaders also frame the agenda of the organization and take major responsibility for organizing political activities. In tandem with the ongoing work of identifying and training leaders, the local IAF organization works on issues. Some of these are very local. For example, a regional subgroup of Valley Interfaith consisting of half a dozen churches in Brownsville might be working to convince the city to open a branch library in their area. Other issues are broader in scope, including the very broad agenda of improving low-wage work. The first living wage campaign in America was driven by the IAF in Baltimore, and, since then, numerous IAF organizations have initiated campaigns. IAF organizations have been aggressive in pushing economic development authorities to link incentives to job quality, and they have implemented a network of job training programs that have won national recognition.[6]

An example of what these groups can accomplish is the work of Valley Interfaith in the Lower Rio Grande Valley.[7] Valley leaders and organizers began to think seriously about a living wage campaign in 1997 after they succeeded in passing a bond authorization and a small sales tax increase to fund the construction of new schools, libraries, and health facilities. Full of energy from this victory, people asked about the wages of the workers who would build the projects. The leaders researched the construction labor market and found that wages in the Valley were so low that many people traveled north to Houston to find more decent pay. They also learned, however, that they faced a legal obstacle in trying to change this situation: according to the Texas attorney general, it would require state enabling legislation to give a municipality the authority to set a wage standard for contractors. Although Valley Interfaith would eventually launch a campaign to attain this legislation as a first step, they decided at this point to examine the wage levels of the school district employees. In each of these districts there were food service workers, cleaners, grounds staff, and bus drivers earning the minimum wage or just above. Because each district was independent, Valley Interfaith needed to work on each school board individually.

Valley Interfaith mobilized large numbers of leaders to attend meetings with school boards and county commissioners; in other instances, small group negotiations worked. In the end, the campaign was a remarkable success. There were three categories of people who benefited from this living wage campaign: people who had their wages raised directly as a result of the campaign, people who were already paid above the living wage but who were given an increase in order to maintain customary differentials, and people who worked in districts that were not targets of the campaign but that raised wages in response to the campaign, either to maintain morale or avoid losing employees. In total, the campaign increased the wages of 7,400 people.[8] More to the point, Valley Interfaith has continued to organize successfully around wage levels in additional school districts and has used the ongoing campaigns as a rallying point around which to build the organization and obtain power to take on other issues, such as the use of economic development subsidies, school reform, and job training.

IAF organizations and other community organizing networks such as PICO (People Improving Communities through Organizing), DART (Direct Action and Research Training), and Gamaliel are major players in many regions and are probably the key complement to unions. But they are not the only vehicle for organizing around job quality. Another variant of a community-based organization is the worker center. Largely focused on low-wage immigrant communities, worker centers offer a range of services, including legal help and pressure on employers. Some are affiliated formally or loosely with unions, but the majority are freestanding. According to Rutgers professor Janice Fine, who has written the leading study, as of 2005 there were 122 worker centers throughout the nation, with the vast majority founded since 1995.[9]

Fine provides a catalog of the achievements of many centers. The Garment Workers Center in Los Angeles forced a clothing brand, Forever 21, to negotiate with it to improve working conditions and wages. The National Day Laborer Organizing Network negotiated with Home Depot to regularize the hiring of day laborers outside of its stores. The Coalition of Immokalee Workers forced Taco Bell and Yum Brands to pressure growers to raise the wages of tomato harvesters in Florida. The Workplace Project in Long Island, New York, led a successful campaign to pass legislation in New York State to strengthen wage and hour enforcement, the Unpaid Wages Prohibition Act. The New York Taxi Workers Alliance won a fare increase from the New York City Council.

Convincing or requiring firms to upgrade the quality of their work requires power. Given that low-wage immigrants are probably the least powerful social group in the nation, how do these centers obtain their power? The Immokalee campaign was based on the threat of a consumer boycott. The Workplace Project engaged in door-to-door political organizing on Long Island. The Garment Workers Center effort relied on picketing and pressure on local politicians.

Another good example is the Restaurant Opportunities Center (ROC) in

New York, which is part of a national network that includes worker centers in Los Angeles, Chicago, Miami, New Orleans, and Washington, D.C. We visited the New York chapter of ROC, which was founded after the September 11 tragedy to help displaced workers find new jobs. It now operates on several fronts to improve low-wage jobs in the city's thriving restaurant industry. One strategy is to run campaigns against high-profile eateries or chains (often with headline celebrity chefs) that violate minimum wage or overtime laws. These campaigns, nine of which had taken place by late 2010, involve lawsuits, picketing, and publicity and, according to the ROC, have netted over $5 million in payments to employees. In addition, the settlement agreements typically include provisions that go beyond adherence to the law, such as improved opportunities for back-of-the-house employees (who tend to be lower-wage) to train for server positions.

The ROC also operates a cooperative restaurant that serves as a training center for members and offers formal courses in a range of cooking and serving skills. Also active on the public policy front, the ROC has introduced legislation regarding tips and paid sick leave. Perhaps the activity with the greatest potential is the Employers Roundtable, a group of restaurants following high-road employment practices in terms of wages, compliance, and advancement opportunities. This roundtable, organized by the ROC, has issued a manual of best practices that the New York City Department of Consumer Affairs published and that all restaurants receive when they apply for a new or renewed license. The motivation of the high-road employers is clear: to avoid being undercut by competitors who lower their costs by squeezing their employees. What is interesting is that the ROC and the city are jointly searching for a strategy to avoid low-wage competition.

What Is the Problem?

The foregoing shows that when unions are in place, they are successful in raising the wages of low earners. In addition, throughout the nation community organizations, interfaith groups, and worker centers have been increasingly active and can boast of numerous local successes. Indeed, the flourishing of these groups is one of the most positive developments in recent years. Given all this, we are now left with a challenge: Why have unions taken such a beating in recent years and been unable to improve the low-wage labor market on the scale that they should be capable of achieving? And why has the overall national impact of all the organizing energy of community groups been so modest?

Turning first to unions, the difficulty is obvious when we look at figures 6.1 and 6.2: only a small fraction of employees are unionized. Indeed, unions are a rapidly declining force in American private-sector employment. The trajectory of this decline is well known: in 1973, unions accounted for 24.2

percent of private-sector employment, and by 2010 the figure had plummeted to 6.9 percent. What is keeping the union movement on life support is the public sector, where 35.9 percent of employees are members, a figure that may well decline sharply as public-sector unions increasingly come under attack in the current political climate.[10]

There is an extensive literature that surveys employees regarding their view of unions, and a strong and consistent finding is that far more people report wishing that they were represented by unions than in fact are.[11] When the well-known pollster Peter Hart asked nonmanagerial employees their preferences in 2005, 55 percent of non-union workers said that they wished that they were represented by a union, and 90 percent of already unionized workers said that they wanted to continue to be represented. Taken together, these responses add up to a desire of about 58 percent of the nonmanagerial workforce for representation, a fraction far in excess of the actual reach of unions. This finding has been replicated in other surveys, although it must also be said that support for unions appears to be eroding. For example, recent surveys by Pew Research and Gallup show that 42 percent of Americans (Pew) and 48 percent (Gallup) approve of unions, figures that are the lowest since 1985.[12] Of course, there is a degree of volatility in these figures, and it also provides context to note that, in the same polls, fewer than half of the respondents had a favorable assessment of corporations. Nonetheless, the downward trend, which is exacerbated by the current criticism of public-sector unions, is unmistakable.

Even taking into account weakening support, far more Americans wish to be represented by unions than are currently represented. What, then, is the problem? There are two issues. The first is that the legal and political deck has been stacked against unions. The second is that unions have contributed to their own decline by failing to organize, by failing to develop an internal democratic culture, by failing to connect effectively with allies, and by appearing to represent the narrow interest of "just another" interest group. Many people in the labor movement recognize these problems, and they are being addressed by some unions, but more progress in addressing these challenges is critical.

When it comes to the law, the process of organizing unions is fundamentally broken. Just how broken it is can be glimpsed in the statistics of success and failure. There are two paths to a union. The first is an agreement between an employer and a union to permit employees to organize without any contestation. This happens on occasion, but it requires that the firm be amenable to both the union and the contract terms; that typically occurs only when the union can generate considerable political support. The more common procedure takes three steps: an organizing drive asking employees to sign a card requesting an election; then, if at least 30 percent sign the card, an election held under the supervision of the National Labor Relations Board; and finally, if a majority votes in favor of the union, an attempt by the union and the employer to reach agreement on a contract. Only with success at this final stage is the union's status secured.

There are no good statistics on what fraction of organizing campaigns result in an election, but Stanford professor John-Paul Ferguson, who has studied the process extensively, puts the figure at about 50 percent.[13] Ferguson does have good data on success in the subsequent stages and finds that only one time in seven does an election result in a signed contract.[14] This is a remarkably low success rate on its own terms, and it is much worse when combined with the 50 percent attrition prior to the election. These outcomes should be compared to the survey data cited earlier on the much larger number of people who want to be represented by a union.

Perhaps this failure rate reflects the lack of interest of employees in being represented, but in fact we saw that many employees would like to join unions. Of course, these polls represent "cheap talk"—when push comes to shove, people may respond differently. Nonetheless, there is overwhelming evidence that concerted and often illegal employer opposition is a central part of the story. An entire industry of consultants has emerged to advise firms on how to beat union-organizing campaigns. In addition, there is good evidence that the rate of illegal efforts to beat unions has also increased. For example, a recent review of National Labor Relations Board records found that the fraction of campaigns that witnessed illegal firing of organizers grew from (an already too high) 16 percent in the 1990s to 26 percent in the 2000s.[15]

Having said all of this, it is also important to ask about the behavior of unions themselves. To a nontrivial extent, they also bear responsibility for their weakening grip on the workforce. Over the course of labor's long decline, many unions stopped organizing new employees and limited themselves to managing contracts. In this role, they came to be seen as just another special interest asking, like any other, for a larger share for their own particular constituency. The growing dominance of this so-called business unionism cost unions their social movement character and also suppressed internal politics and leadership development.[16] In addition, and related to the foregoing, too many unions became the preserve of middle-aged white men and hence had difficulties connecting with the new workforce as it was developing. At the local level, many unions were resistant to working with other community organizations. The unions preferred to hoard their own power and access and also saw community groups as either too flaky or too left-wing. As one community organizer commented to us when we talked about cooperation between unions and community groups with respect to green jobs (the topic of chapter 8): "There are going to be a ton of community groups that are going to say there are too many decades, centuries of racism in unions, good old white boy networks, there's no way we're even going to think about going union." What this added up to was not just a decline in the fraction of the workforce represented by unions but also a growing estrangement between unions and other members of a potential progressive coalition.

In important parts of the union movement this is changing. At the level of broad policy, unions no longer view low-wage immigrants as a group of workers who are depressing wages but rather as workers who need their services and whom they can organize. Some unions now see low-wage immigrants as their primary constituency. In addition to the building worker campaigns, SEUI also organized over sixty thousand home health care workers in California through a combination of traditional organizing and political action in the state legislature. On the East Coast, SEIU has had comparable success in the health care industry, a large employer of low-wage workers. Other unions, such as the Hotel Employees and Restaurant Employees (HERE) and the garment workers' union (UNITE), have also succeeded in new organizing drives that have put new life into the movement. Even in traditional industries, unions seem to have rediscovered their moral voice. For example, the Teamsters' strike against United Parcel Service focused on the issues of part-time and contingent employment and obtained surprisingly broad support from the American public.

Of course, there are still problems, and to see the challenges we return to the Justice for Janitors campaign. The version of the story we told earlier painted that campaign as a triumphant merger of civil rights and community organizing with traditional union bargaining, and there is truth to that version. But there are complexities. First, similar campaigns have not always been successful. Kyoung-Hee Yu studied several JfJ campaigns, including Los Angeles but also the far less successful one in Washington, D.C.[17] In Washington, the campaign faltered in part because of tension between the African American community and the Latino-oriented organizing effort, but to a greater extent because of the organizational style of SEIU. To confront large national employers, SEIU has consolidated its locals into what might be termed megalocals. For example, all building service workers on the East Coast south of Rhode Island are part of one local based in New York City. This has the effect of diminishing membership involvement and leadership development and hence depriving the organization of the kind of social movement fervor that animated the Los Angeles campaign.

This organizational strategy can be defended as necessary given the national footprint of employers, but it also runs the risk of leading the union into a trap that has been highlighted for nearly a century by social scientists—the so-called iron law of oligarchy. This "law" refers to the tendency of organizational leaders to centralize their power, with the consequence that the membership becomes distant and alienated and the organization loses energy and forgets its mission. The extent to which the SEIU is following this track is unclear, but the mixed success of JfJ does raise red flags.

An additional point about the Los Angeles campaign is that, to an extent often unrecognized, its success depended on political power that unions today find slipping from their grasp. In Los Angeles at the time of the campaign, union leadership had a seat on the board of the city's Community Redevelopment Authority, the body whose approval was necessary for all new building projects. This provided unions with leverage on developers, who in turn were able to pressure building owners to settle. As union political power slips, so goes the success of organizing efforts. A related issue is that JfJ in Los Angeles was able to draw on a strong Latino culture and political history of mobilization going back to César Chávez and the farm labor strikes. This provided a unique context that is difficult to replicate elsewhere.

Moving Forward

How can we make progress in strengthening employee voice? There are three components to a convincing answer to this question: unions need to improve their own culture and style of operations; the law needs to change so that unions have a fairer shake; and unions and community groups need to come together in more effective coalitions.

One aspect of unions improving their own culture is the degree to which they are internally democratic and open to new voices. In all fairness, there have been important moves in this direction. Unions have come to understand that their most promising source of growth is found in the low-wage labor market, and some have changed their traditional practices to reach that market. For example, when we interviewed members of the Carpenters Union in Las Vegas, they described modifications in their traditional seniority provisions that enable new, typically minority, workers to stand a chance of bidding on good commercial jobs, whereas in the past they would have been last in a long line of older white carpenters. In New Jersey, the Laborers Union has cooperated in starting a community-based workers center to attract people who otherwise would have never been approached by the union.[18] This is all good, but there needs to be much more progress in order to recapture the social-movement spirit of employee organization.

Consider the comment by Elaine Bernard, the longtime director of the Harvard Trade Union Program and a strong advocate for unions. When asked what unions need to do to survive, she replied: "The answer has to be something that appeals to the individual worker, provides some service to the employer, and promotes a collective community good."[19] Thought of in these terms, unions have a considerable way to go. Unions are not seen as a carrier of a message and platform that speaks to the common interest, but rather as advocates of the narrow self-interest of their members.

An important element of speaking to the public interest is finding ways to work with firms to help them become more competitive. The same surveys that demonstrate that support for unionism is far more widespread than is reflected in their membership figures also show that employees want a form of union that is less adversarial than in the past and more helpful for firm success. The evidence is quite strong that when unions and firms do work together both sides benefit, and unions need to become more open to this kind of relationship. An example of effective win-win relationships can be found in health care. On the West Coast, the Kaiser health system has improved its performance by working with its unions, and on the East Coast, local 1199 in New York and 1199C in Philadelphia have worked very effectively with employers. These models need to be extended.

It does, however, take two to tango, and this brings us to the issue of labor law reform. As things stand now, too many employers find it much too easy to evade unions through legal—and sometimes illegal—campaigns and foot-dragging. We saw the consequences of this in the discussion of the dismal success of organizing campaigns. The law needs to be reformed to create a more even playing field. Unions pushed hard in the first year of the Obama administration for legislation creating a card check system that had the potential of avoiding election campaigns. In retrospect, making this proposal the centerpiece of labor legislation was probably a mistake; a more nuanced reform package could well have been passed and signed by the president. Nevertheless, the case for labor law reform remains strong and is the second leg of any strategy for moving forward.

The third leg of the strategy is to bring unions and community groups into a stronger and more durable relationship. Worker centers offer a strategy for improving employment in the myriad small and medium-size firms that are effectively out of the reach of unions because of the difficulty of organizing dispersed worksites and because labor law, which requires 51 percent victories in elections, poses significant obstacles in these settings. However, worker centers are small and scattered and operate at a scale that pales relative to the workforce whom they serve and the firms with which they must deal. Janice Fine reports that over half have budgets of less than $250,000 and that three-quarters have memberships of less than one thousand workers.[20]

The IAF's emphasis on leadership development, broad-based organizing, and incorporation of values offers key insights about how to move ahead. In addition, the IAF approach of organizing through churches and schools can be very helpful when workplaces are small and scattered and people are in temporary or contingent employment with high turnover. In these circumstances, traditional union workplace-based organizing is both difficult and expensive. Workers can more effectively be reached in other settings and subsequently brought together around employment concerns.

This model points the way toward a strategy for revitalizing larger and more potentially powerful unions. What the IAF can bring to unions is captured well by the labor historian Nelson Lichtenstein, a very sympathetic observer of the union movement:

> The unions need tens of thousands of new organizers; but the AFL-CIO cannot recruit, train, and deploy such an army, and even if it could, "organizers" who parachute into a campaign are far less effective than those who are part of the community and the workplace. Such a homegrown cadre cannot be recruited in the absence of a democratic, participatory union culture. Unfortunately, thousands of local unions, and not a few national or international organizations, are job trusts that exist to protect the incomes of a strata of long-service officials . . . but without that democratization the union movement will remain a shell.[21]

The IAF model of leadership development can generate the kind of energy that has been too often lacking in organized labor.

In addition, the IAF and other organizations could work together in coalitions aimed at pressuring firms to offer better-quality jobs. Indeed, in a number of cities, IAF organizations and unions have begun working together to this end. The nation's first living wage campaign was the product of a joint effort by the IAF organization in Baltimore (BUILD) and the public employees union. In Los Angeles, the IAF has worked closely with the SEIU and HERE on a number of campaigns. Immigration rights is an issue that resonates powerfully for both the IAF and the unions in that city. In Phoenix and Omaha, the IAF has worked with the Food and Commercial Workers Union in several new organizing campaigns.

The IAF, of course, is not the only game in town. Throughout the country there are many community groups working on employment issues. In chapter 8, we describe the actions of community organizations in Boston and Portland as they organized to ensure that newly funded "green" jobs came with decent wages and were connected to opportunities for upward mobility. We will see that their success was mixed, largely because of the difficulty of obtaining local and federal political support, but the fact is that in each of these cities, and elsewhere, there is a dense network of active and committed organizations that do move policy in the right direction. A truly effective strategy to build employee voice would bring these networks together with unions in an effective coalition of equal and mutually respectful partners.

Conclusion

We cannot make progress on raising employment quality without having the capacity to put pressure on firms and on government. Without that pressure, there simply is neither constituency nor incentive to move forward. The

question, then, is how to build the necessary power, and this chapter has focused on two main actors: unions and community groups. Certainly unions
have to be at the heart of any national coalition, or even regional coalition,
but they cannot achieve what is necessary on their own. Other players are
important, both for the assets they bring to the effort and for the lessons they
offer to unions on how to organize.

CHAPTER 7

Working with Firms to Upgrade Work

Anchoring the Boston economy are the world-class hospitals that, taken together, amount to the largest source of jobs in the region. Add to these numerous nursing homes and other health facilities, and the importance of this sector to the region is obvious. Researchers, doctors, and highly skilled nurses are central to delivering quality health care and world-class innovation, but they are not alone in these efforts. Just as is true throughout the country, a large low-paid workforce labors at the core of the industry: the kitchen staff, the orderlies, the cleaners, the certified nursing assistants, the patient care technicians, the laundry workers, and many others without whom the system would break down. These people come from all parts of the world and speak different languages, but they do have two things in common: they work very hard, and they are poorly paid. Nevertheless, they work in an industry that provides one of the very best examples of what can be done in cooperation with employers to improve the quality of low-wage jobs.

In the spring of 2010, a graduation was held in the auditorium of Children's Hospital for employees from several hospitals who had just finished a program supported by their employers and several foundations and managed by Jewish Vocational Services (JVS). Some had completed the final step in the "English for Speakers of Other Languages" program, and others had completed a college bridge program aimed at getting them ready to enter a community college. Attending beside the employees were their families, program staff, and hospital managers. It was a happy and proud event, and the most moving talks were given by employees who spoke about how hard they had worked, how they could not have achieved what they had without the program's support, and the jobs or education they hoped to move into next. For these people it was clear that bad jobs were being transformed into better ones.

Jewish Vocational Services is a large agency that operates a wide range of education and training programs in the Boston area. It works with the Russian Jewish immigrant community to facilitate their settling in the area. It has a program with CVS Pharmacy to help people from the community obtain entry-level sales jobs and then, with enough luck and ambition, move into positions like pharmacy technicians. JVS is beginning to work with a local community organization with roots in the Haitian community to establish a college preparatory program for adults. But its largest effort is with health care employers. The spring 2010 graduation at Children's Hospital was for employees in multiple hospitals in the area, but JVS also works with nursing homes. These employers have an even higher proportion of low-wage workers because of the nature of the business, which is largely daily care and maintenance of elderly residents.

All of the organizations with which JVS collaborates speak highly of the quality of their instruction, but the impact of this agency's work goes beyond good teaching. In a variety of ways, JVS has enhanced what might be termed the "education and training" culture within the employers. It accomplishes this partly by encouraging small but significant changes in policies, such as when it worked with Children's Hospital to enable prepayment of tuition assistance, a change that opened up opportunities for people whose family budgets could not accommodate tuition bills. JVS also hosts monthly meetings with the human resources staff of all its client employers and in these sessions diffuses best practices. In some organizations, JVS has innovated in pedagogy—for example, by shifting its ESOL (English for Speakers of Other Languages) teaching away from chalk-and-talk and toward experiential activities. This led to greater success rates, which in turn encouraged the organizations to expand the amount of training that they provided their employees. In addition, because JVS is an important actor operating at some scale, it can effectively link employers to other actors, such as community colleges or state funding agencies. In short, our interviews with health care providers elicited convincing testimony that the amount of training they provide to their employees has increased owing to their relationships with JVS.

JVS is not alone in working to improve job quality in the health care industry. We visited several hospitals and nursing homes in Philadelphia that are part of a very large career ladder and training program rooted in a collective bargaining agreement with union local 1199C. The program is funded by a contribution from the employers set at 1.5 percent of the wage bill and is organized and managed by the union in cooperation with the employers. Unlike many career ladder efforts, this one is large enough to merit its own facility—a cheerful building in the city's downtown.

A total of over eleven thousand employees pass annually through this program for services that range from the simple processing of tuition assistance payments to assessment (such as GED testing) and a broad range of classes. Over three thousand employees are in education or training programs. Employees in low-level positions (cleaners, orderlies, LPNs who wish to become RNs, and so on) are given some released time and tuition assistance by their employer, and the counselors and faculty at the program assist them in meeting the education requirements needed to move up.

One woman told us that she had wanted to be a nurse but was discouraged by a college counselor. She had dropped out of school, passed through a series of casual jobs, and then landed employment as a nurse's aide. She connected with the program and entered LPN training, achieved that, and was now in an RN program part-time while working. We also met a young man who was, in his words, "educated on the street." He had heard about the assessment center, came in, did the foundation courses, became a CNA, and was now in an LPN program. His friends told us that during a major snowstorm he had walked three miles to get to work because he felt he had made a commitment. Another woman we met was a ninth-grade dropout who had entered through the GED program.

The 1199C program operates on a scale that dwarfs any effort not associated with a union, and its success is clearly related to the scale it can achieve, its stable funding due to the automatic set-aside, and the power it wields. Many of the other programs that we visited were much smaller and focused on identifying a cohort of ten to thirty employees per year, providing them with a career coach and tuition assistance, and guiding them through the process into a better job. One way to achieve scale is a tactic used by the Baltimore Alliance for Careers in Health Care, a foundation-supported effort to diffuse career ladders in the Baltimore region. This organization aggregates demand across hospitals so that there is sufficient size to mount a training program. For instance, when aggregated across employers, a training program for incumbent employees to become unit clerks and surgical techs, two occupations for which each hospital had a few openings, could be organized.

Another example of career ladder programs in hospitals is the CNA–nurse extender–patient care ladder at Good Samaritan Hospital in Baltimore. The program was developed by hospital staff in response to high turnover and shortages of CNAs, and it is also supported by the Baltimore Alliance. As of the spring of 2009, nearly three hundred new CNAs had been trained in the program, of whom 60 percent were incumbent employees in lower-level positions. These employees received release time for the training, although CNAs who wish to continue to climb the ladder have to undertake the training on their own time, a policy that seems to reflect less urgency among senior hospital staff regarding turnover and shortages. The staff at Good Samaritan reported a very high demand among employees for the program.

All of these efforts to improve job quality fall under the rubric of "career ladders"—programs aimed at improving opportunities for upward mobility within firms. At its most ambitious, a career ladder program works with employers to create new rungs on a job ladder and then provides training to low-wage employees to help them make that climb. A less ambitious, but possibly more realistic, strategy is to find ways to help firms augment the amount of training that low-wage workers receive, with the expectation that extra training will enable them to climb the already existing job ladder within the firm.

Why would firms want to participate in these programs? Our earlier discussion about carrots and sticks points to the answer. Health care providers suffer from high turnover, and some also experience labor shortages in the technician positions that are often targets of these programs. So employers benefit from their employees' higher level of commitment and effort, as well as from a lower turnover rate and the associated reduced costs of recruitment. At the same time, health care providers are vulnerable to pressure to improve jobs. This is obvious in the case of employers with union contracts but is also true more generally. Hospitals and other providers are quasi-public in the sense that even private ones rely very heavily on public funding and hence are sensitive to pressure. Their reliance on numerous regulatory decisions also helps make them responsive to these programs. In addition, the shape of the job structure is such that multiple levels of employment—for example, numerous technician jobs—represent reasonable targets for the upward advancement of low-wage workers. For these reasons, more career ladder programs can be found in health care than in any other industry.

Job Training and Upward Mobility

Thus far we have described what is possible, but now we want to step back and address a misconception that might block action: the belief of some observers that it is not possible to mount public training programs that have any degree of success with low-wage or low-skill workers. Much of this criticism is aimed at programs that are external to the firm, and it is reasonable to think that firm-based training and programs upgraded for incumbent workers will have greater success owing to their grounding in the needs of employers. But is it really true that public training is guaranteed to fail? In fact, well-designed programs can have substantial success.

We saw in chapter 3 that vocational training in community colleges has a substantial payoff. What about the myriad programs funded by public second-chance job training programs? These efforts have a long history, beginning with the War on Poverty and moving through various incarnations at the federal level and governance changes in cities and states. In addition to federal funding, innovative and effective efforts have been supported by foundations as well as by business associations and unions.

Careful evaluations of specific programs support the point that real training investments pay off. One example is the random assignment evaluation of three "sectoral" programs—that is, programs that provide entry-level training in specific industries (in this case, health care, manufacturing, and information technology) for people who have multiple barriers to employment and who averaged less than $10,000 in annual earnings prior to the program.[1] After completion of the program, the treatment group earned over $4,000 more than the control group.

Another powerful example is Project QUEST in San Antonio, Texas. This program has several features that are consistent with what has come to be seen as best practice. It works with employers to identify future job needs and often involves employers in designing training, and it provides a good deal of support to trainees in the form of counseling and small amounts of financial assistance. Project QUEST is relatively long-term and hence makes real investments in people. One participant whom we interviewed said that "they believed in me and made me feel ten feet tall," while another said that "there was opportunity at a time when I needed a lifeline." Evaluation results support these observations: participants gained nearly $5,000 yearly relative to a comparison group.[2] Similar results were found for a sister program in Austin called Capital Idea.[3]

Taken as a whole, these evaluations should be seen as "existence proofs" that well-designed training can be effective. The point is that for training programs, as with other policies, there is a distribution of outcomes, and too often the discussion ignores evidence that success is possible. Rather than giving up, we should learn best-practice lessons and aspire toward these. This has happened in the charter school debate, where a broad range of advocates focus on best-practice cases rather than on the outcomes in the average program, and there is no reason why the same attitude should not prevail for job training.

Career Ladders

Health care providers are an attractive venue for training and career ladder programs because they provide many middle-level job opportunities that low-wage workers can aspire to and because they are more vulnerable than many other employers to public pressure to play ball. That being said, there have been significant initiatives in other industries, and here we describe several in hotels and in manufacturing.

Hotels represent a greater challenge than health care because of the nature of the jobs. There is a large low-wage base of room cleaners as well as laundry and kitchen workers. The problem is that there are proportionally fewer jobs in the middle level of the organization to which these workers can aspire. Nonetheless, because so many low-wage workers are employed in hotels, there have been a number of efforts to provide training opportunities for incumbent workers and to open career pathways for them.

We described in chapter 6 the hotel training and career ladder program created by the Culinary Workers Union in Las Vegas. Was that effort unique in that it depended on the special circumstances of Las Vegas and the relationship of the union to large employers in that city? Another union-based program, this one in Boston, provides some reassurance that this is not the case.

The Boston hotels program was organized by the local union Unite HERE local 25, which represented over half of the eleven thousand hotel workers in Boston.[4] In 2004, the union created an on-call banquet-server training in which longtime servers trained other union members so that they could pick up extra shifts during busy periods. The union negotiated with the hotels to ensure that the spots would first be offered to members who had gone through the training. Once the banquet training was established, the union worked with hotel managers to determine whether there were other needs that a union-run training program could fill. A training program was opened to union members in 2006, and in 2008 additional funds from the state Workforce Competitiveness Trust Fund led to the formation of the Hotel Training Workforce Partnership. This funding and structure allows training to be provided to people seeking entry into jobs at union hotels as well as to incumbent workers, who are trained in general skills such as computers and English language. Working with the hotels, the union has developed a professional busser–food server certificate. Additionally, the program offers certification courses in food safety and the handling of alcohol. Across all of its components, the program served 267 union members in 2007 and 416 in 2008.

These training and certificate programs, combined with guidance from a career coach, are intended to create several career pathways within union hotels. Program managers have developed these pathways by working with union and hotel managers to identify competencies and evaluation criteria for different positions within three departments: food and beverage, guest services, and culinary.

These career pathways are relatively new, and it is too soon to tell whether they have made an impact on the hotels' promotion practices. Nevertheless, the general response to the program has been good. All of the human resource managers we spoke with felt that the program has been responsive to the needs of the hotels. One manager reported that the program had "been a win all around," with no unforeseen costs. No one felt that it was time-consuming to work with the program. "The relationship has been far better than any of us could have imagined."

Programs for incumbent workers in manufacturing have a different feel than those in hotels or health care. The focus is less on upward mobility and more on upgrading the skills of incumbent workers and providing technical assistance to firms so that they can operate more efficiently. This latter emphasis is driven by the difficult economic circumstances of manufacturing enterprises, which are much more at risk than health care providers or hotels.

Another key difference is that manufacturing programs focus much more on small and medium-size firms that lack the internal capacity to think systematically about their human resource needs. An example of a sustained effort to work with small manufacturers to improve the training and advancement opportunities of low-wage employees is the Retention and Advancement Demonstration Program, which was managed nationally between 2001 and 2004 by the National Association of Manufacturers and locally in three states by state-level employers' associations in Connecticut, Michigan, and Pennsylvania.[5]

The associations that worked with the employers were consistently struck by the poor quality and stressed-out nature of the human resource (HR) systems they encountered and by the limited expectations that HR staff and supervisors held out for entry-level or low-wage workers. An important part of the effort was attempting to change both of these facts. With respect to the HR systems, a staff person in one of the business associations commented, "Even though company managers usually expressed their top priority as skills upgrading, we usually had to work our way toward the frontline workforce, fixing up various HR systems along the way. It would do little good, and probably be impossible anyway, to mount effective training initiatives if the underlying HR systems and supervisory practices wouldn't support or take advantage of such efforts." This observation speaks directly to the point made in chapter 4: the suboptimal nature of the operation of many firms and the scope for improvement. This is a central point because it shows that there is room for productivity gains that can benefit low-wage employees as well as the employers.

Once the HR systems were in place, the local associations either provided training or brokered it. The topics included business writing, blueprint reading, quality control, customer relations–customer service, basic plant metrics, statistical process control, laser technology, plastics molding, machinist skills, lean manufacturing, continuous improvement, Adobe Photoshop and Illustrator, process certification, basic computer skills, and English as a Second Language (ESL).

Challenges

Both the large union-based 1199C program and the smaller non-union interventions have run up against a set of challenges. In the case of 1199C, resistance has flowed from the affiliation with the union. For example, the University of Pennsylvania medical system's refusal to work with the program seems to stem from a reluctance to let the union in the door, even in this capacity. However, there has also been a resistance stemming from broader-based managerial attitudes that was reflected in many of the non-union programs we visited. The twin problems are skepticism about training and the problem that the players in the organization—senior management, the human resource department, program operators, and line supervisors—are often not on the same page.

An example of managerial skepticism emerged in a conversation with the head of a nursing home that was part of a chain. This leader worked with the 1199C program (even though he was non-union) and by creating some career paths had reduced turnover of CNAs from 60 percent to 10 percent. Yet despite this success, he was unable to convince his colleagues, that is, the leaders of other nursing homes in the organization, to participate. He attributed this failure to inertia and to a lack of belief in training for this population of employees.

Within the larger non-union hospitals the resistance tends to be found in the human resource departments and among some line supervisors. The advocates are senior management, who have a strong interest in community relations, and the program staff. However, the HR staff are often committed to their own routines of recruitment and assessment, and supervisors are focused on what is easiest in terms of staffing (which is often hiring from the outside) as opposed to creating opportunities for lower-level employees to move up. Why does senior management not simply insist on cooperation and execution? The answer lies in the multiple pressures and interests of top management. Although these leaders appear to have a genuine interest in the programs, they also confront myriad other problems, and forcing their middle managers out of their routines in order to create career ladders or expand training opportunities is often seen as relatively low-priority and disruptive, no matter how much top management likes the idea in principle. Hence, the programs remain relatively small-scale in the larger organizational context.

An additional challenge these programs face stems from how hard it is for many employees to obtain the education and skills that it takes to move up job ladders in hospitals. Virtually all of the target jobs require at least a community college–level certificate, and many require a two-year degree. The unfortunate reality is that many, if not most, of the employees aspiring to move out of low-wage jobs have something like an eighth-grade educational attainment, and many also face challenges with English. In addition, workers' family circumstances can pose significant obstacles. Put in terms of our earlier discussions, there are clear human capital challenges as well as organizational and structural barriers to the success of job ladders, and it is naive to deny or ignore this. The consequence is that the path from, say, working in the kitchen to working as a CNA to getting an LPN or tech job can take five or more years. This is a long haul, and many do not make it.

Several of the manufacturing programs described earlier were evaluated, at least via careful narratives if not formal random assignment. The National Association of Manufacturers program described earlier involved one thousand employees, and according to the evaluation report, a total of twenty-eight salary increases and fourteen promotions were attributed to the program. These low outcomes numbers were supplemented by the evaluator's opinion that the program also improved the overall operation of the firms and hence held out the prospect of more employee gains going forward. This view was supported by numerous comments by the employers praising the effort and pointing to the gains that they experienced. Although these observations are optimistic, it is important to acknowledge the very limited measurable gains to employees after an intervention that lasted three full years.

A second assessment comes from a program that began in 2002 in Massachusetts aimed at working with firms to increase training and develop career paths for low-skill and low-wage incumbent workers in three industries: health care, financial services, and manufacturing.[6] More than two thousand employees were involved, slightly over 40 percent of them in manufacturing. The program devoted substantial resources to working with employers in designing career pathways and providing training to employees. As the evaluation noted, "With its emphasis on incumbent workers, career pathways, integrated curricula and employer involvement, [the initiative] incorporated new 'best practices' of workforce development into program design." Given the substantial resources and the best-practice design and execution, this effort represents a good test of the model; as it turns out, the outcomes were quite mixed. The bottom line is that employers displayed very little interest in developing career ladders and, when the program staff laid out possible pathways, very little interest in implementing them. The evaluators commented:

> It remains unclear whether limited demand for career path models across industry sectors is due to lack of information (i.e., employers are simply unfamiliar with the concept and need better/more information about career path models), lack of time and resources (i.e., employers don't have the internal resources to develop and implement the approach) or due to employer perceptions regarding entry-level workers (i.e., employers have difficulty viewing entry-level workers as future skilled labor).

The experience was more positive with respect to training. Both employers and employees were happy to receive additional training resources and to participate in the programs. It turned out that the level of basic skills needs was considerably higher than expected, and in the end over half of all training resources went into ESL skills and other basic skills subjects rather than training more directly aimed at job-related skills. The implication was that even if career paths were created, there was going to be a long haul involved in moving people up through them. In addition, interviews with employees showed that many of them were interested in the ESL and other basic skills training as a pathway to improving the quality of their lives and their self-confidence rather than in terms of career advancement.

A final, and somewhat discouraging, finding is that although employers expressed satisfaction with the training, they also explicitly cited as a major reason the fact that the program was costless to them. The firms did not continue making the training available when the subsidy ended. Looking on the more positive side, however, we note that as long as the training was subsidized, employers were willing to let public programs through their doors, something that is not always easy to accomplish. Reports of similar efforts in other parts of the country also demonstrate that involving employers in subsidized training interventions is quite feasible.[7]

Conclusion

One way of interpreting the results reported in this chapter is to conclude that the career ladder idea is flawed. The basis for this view is that there is very little evidence in any of the cases that new job paths have been created that operate at any scale. That is, firms have not fundamentally reorganized their promotion ladders in order to create new "rungs" (new jobs or reconfigured tasks) that enable low-wage workers to move up more easily. This would be a possible reading, but it is too pessimistic. Ladders may not have been reshaped, but employers have been encouraged, incentivized, and supported in increasing the amount of training that they provide to their incumbent workforce. This is clear in the work of JVS in Boston, 1199C in Philadelphia, and the several hotel projects we reviewed, and (to a lesser extent) in the manufacturing examples. This is important for two reasons. First, as we have seen, one of the markers of bad jobs is that they provide little training. We saw this in the data that demonstrated that low-wage workers receive far less firm-based training than do their more-advantaged colleagues. Increasing training is also important because it enables employees to move up existing job paths. Even if the job paths remain the same, more training can improve the prospects of those at the bottom, and in this sense the nature of low-level jobs changes. Instead of being dead-end, they now lead somewhere.

The path to progress is not easy. The internal politics of organizations can be problematic. Multiple organizational actors—top executives, HR staff, line supervisors, the staff charged with running the programs—have different priorities, and these are not always congruent. We also saw that small employers often lack the managerial capacity or human resource staff to take full advantage of the programs. On top of all this, these programs take a long time. The difficulties faced by low-wage workers, in terms of both acquiring skills and dealing with family issues, makes it a long haul for them to get the training they need and move up the job ladder. It is naive to expect easy and rapid improvements.

But there are more positive lessons. Virtually all employees involved in the programs are eager participants. Their motivation and desire to improve themselves is very strong and provides a strong basis for moving forward. We also saw that the programs that work best have one of several organizational characteristics: they are linked to a union, they work via a business association, or they are managed by a large sophisticated nonprofit. Finally, it does seem clear that well-designed programs can help change the culture of organizations and move them toward seeing the training and education of low-wage workers as a good way of doing business. This is an important step forward in improving the quality of these jobs.

In sum, career ladders and training programs deserve to be viewed as one element in any effort to improve job quality. Even as they move us down the path and accomplish a good deal, however, it is still important to improve wages through some of the more direct strategies discussed in previous chapters. And as noted several times, these more direct pressures strengthen the commitment of firms to training and improving the upward mobility of their workforces.

CHAPTER 8

Job Quality on the Ground: The Story of Green Jobs*

The core argument of this book is that there are choices when it comes to job quality and that low-wage work need not be low-quality. We have discussed the ideas that make this point plausible and described policies that hold promise in getting us there. But how do the necessary choices actually get made? What are the politics and decisions at play? These questions can be asked and at least partially answered in the abstract, but it would be very helpful to observe the process in real time. In this chapter, we focus on the emergence—or more accurately, the sudden rapid growth—of a new occupation and the struggles around the question of what these jobs will be like.

Weatherization jobs grew rapidly because of funding in the American Recovery and Reinvestment Act of 2009 (the so-called stimulus bill or Recovery Act). Additional impetus came from a broader interest in green jobs, which led to a range of initiatives at the state level. Because weatherization jobs are relatively new, their wages, working conditions, and career structure are up for grabs and subject to debate and choice. The word "choice" is key here. There are multiple players who have views about the appropriate nature of weatherization work, and they have been active in pushing their perspectives. Just what these jobs look like in the end will be the result of these political struggles. Market considerations—supply and demand and skill—will certainly play a role in shaping outcomes, but so will the capacities of the various players as they maneuver to get their way.

The political contest over the shape of weatherization jobs is especially relevant for the concerns of this book. Weatherization workers are typical of employees in many low-wage jobs in America. They are blue-collar, often immigrants, and often poorly paid. The work is relatively unskilled, and there is

*Co-authored with Elizabeth Chimienti

no shortage of people wanting to do it; hence, the forces of supply and demand in the job market exert a strong downward pressure on wages. However, when the work is funded by federal dollars or through funds taken from ratepayers and under the control of regulated utilities, there is ample opportunity for the "visible hand" to shape the nature of the job. A great deal of employment, far more than might be understood, has this character. The entire health care system is quasi-public and is staffed by millions of low-paid employees. Public authorities contract for construction projects and thus can help set the nature of working conditions. Governments buy goods and in principle can exert their influence on the nature of work for those who produce those goods. Every day, cities and towns negotiate zoning exemptions or economic development deals, all of which offer opportunities to shape jobs.

Numerous progressive groups have sensed the opening provided by the recent spurt of green jobs funding. Their struggles and challenges tell us a lot about what is possible. To shed light on these issues, we conducted extensive interviews—in Boston, Portland, Houston, and at the national level—with individuals and organizations who have sought to shape the nature of and access to weatherization work.

The bottom line is complex. The broadest ambitions of advocates pushing for high-quality jobs have rarely been realized. The new funding and the effort to shape the employment conditions of weatherization work have had virtually no impact on the much larger residential construction job market, but given the relative size of these markets, this is not surprising. What is more unexpected is that the surge in funding and the new regulations have only partially transformed even the more narrowly defined weatherization field. The variable strength of progressive coalitions, legislative politics, and timing all contributed to the development of an uneven set of regulations at the federal and local levels. Groups that are putative allies have often worked at cross-purposes. More strikingly, government at both the local and federal levels has been conservative and even timid about establishing job standards. There are also more positive lessons. Training standards are being formalized, to the benefit of both homeowners and workers. Although there have been conflicts, it is also true that interests that historically were at each other's throats—notably unions and community groups—have found a way to work together more constructively than in the past. Weatherization work, while not what one might hope, has been somewhat improved.

These complexities are important, but the fundamental lesson is fairly stark. While all the players professed to be interested in job quality, it was not priority number one for many of them and frequently got lost in the maneuvering. To make progress on job quality, strong public leadership is essential, and this leadership was present in only a few cities and muted in the case of the federal government. Local politics are important, but the bottom line is that without a clear federal government position and a strong set of federal standards, the pace of progress is slow and very uneven and unlikely to have a broad national impact.

Some Background: Green Jobs and the Stimulus

Residential weatherization means conducting an energy audit on a home and then engaging (if necessary) in relatively straightforward improvements such as installing insulation, filling gaps in structures where heat can escape, and wrapping appliances. On average, these improvements can save a household close to $400 a year in energy costs.[1]

When it comes to job quality, weatherization work is much like residential construction in general. It is overwhelmingly non-union. Only about 16 percent of all construction workers are unionized, and they are found almost entirely in the commercial and public construction sectors. Furthermore, the residential construction sector is dominated by small contractors that often have only three or four employees. Indeed, 65 percent of all construction firms have fewer than five employees, and 91 percent have fewer than twenty.[2] Although it is true that in new residential construction large national firms sit atop subcontractors, in remodeling in general and weatherization in particular the small contractors run the show. As one knowledgeable observer commented: "The vendors . . . are small [contractors] that primarily do sporadic house-by-house work, so they're not to scale, and they don't provide good standards on wages and benefits, and career pipelines. They're small businesses just getting by."

There are few barriers to entry in this industry, and a large fraction of costs is payroll. At the entry level, it takes only about six to eight weeks to train a weatherization installer.[3] These factors lead to considerable pressure on wages. The Bureau of Labor Statistics found that the hourly rate of weatherization workers—generally between $13 and $15 an hour, with benefits variable—is about 40 percent below that of carpenters in the residential sector.[4]

The federal government has subsidized weatherization for low-income households at a relatively low level since 1976. The Weatherization Assistance Program (WAP) was funded by the Department of Energy and typically was administered in localities by community action agencies, the social service agencies that often have their roots in the War on Poverty of the 1960s. This program focused on upgrading homes, paid very little attention to job quality issues, and was not subject to the federal Davis-Bacon Act requirements regarding wages (discussed later in the chapter).

With the stimulus, annual funding for the Weatherization Assistance Program exploded from $450 million a year to $5 billion over three years. The stimulus bill also funded the Energy Efficiency and Conservation Block Grant (EECBG) program to the tune of $3.2 billion. Among other activities, states and cities could use these funds to weatherize the homes of moderate- and higher-income households. All of this funding was in addition to existing state programs, such as the ratepayer-funded utility programs that subsidize residential retrofit work. By the winter of 2009, weatherization had been transformed from a relatively small patchwork of programs to a federal priority. In addition to saving energy, Vice President Joe Biden's Middle Class Task Force expected green jobs to "provide a sustainable family wage, health and retirement benefits, and decent working conditions" and "be available to diverse workers from across the spectrum of race, gender and ethnicity."[5] This was not a description of the existing industry. To meet these goals, something would have to change.

THE PLAYERS AND THEIR ISSUES

When it comes to job quality and weatherization, three broad issues are important. The most obvious issue is wages and benefits. An additional issue is whether the jobs provide training and career ladders so that employees can move up the construction skills and pay ladder. Looked at in isolation, many weatherization jobs are not particularly highly skilled, yet at least in principle these jobs could be the first step on a ladder leading to construction union apprenticeship programs or to skilled work in the largely non-union residential sector. In either case, there would need to be a conscious effort to make these connections. The third issue concerns access: who will get these jobs? At a time of high unemployment, this question is obviously of considerable interest. Advocates take two main points of view: one sees these jobs as the first rung of a career ladder for unemployed people who live in low-income, often minority communities, and the other sees them as temporary work for skilled but unemployed construction workers. It is not surprising that a broad range of organizations have been active in offering their answers to all these questions and in seeking to persuade those holding the purse strings to agree with them.

Comprising one important set of players are members of what might be termed a progressive coalition who are concerned in varying degrees with job quality and access. These groups have more in common than not, but there are clear tensions among them. Organizations such as Green for All and Emerald Cities care about job quality, but they are especially interested in directing work to inner-city, typically minority communities. Construction unions and their allies care about job quality, but they tend to be most responsive to the needs of their unemployed members, who may need to obtain weatherization jobs for the time being. Some unions, notably the Laborers and the Carpenters, also view organizing weatherization work as a strategy for getting a foot in the door of the largely unorganized residential construction market. Lurking in the background is a long history of distrust between historically white construction unions and minority communities that have felt excluded from the good jobs controlled by these unions.

Another set of organizations places less emphasis on the quality of the jobs and more on the number of homes weatherized. In the years before the stimulus, much of the Weatherization Assistance Program flowed through community action agencies, the local social services agencies that provide multiple services in low-income communities. In spite of the surge in funding, representatives from these organizations often express concern that if wages rise substantially, fewer homes will be retrofitted, an outcome they see as contrary to the mission of their program. In addition, the same history of distrust between unions and community groups shapes the attitude of many community action agencies toward unions. Moreover, they view other organizations' new interest in their program with deep suspicion, and they have also seen their budgets surge before, only to be cut severely years later. These factors contribute to their reluctance to hire new workers or set standards that are viable today but may be infeasible in the long run.

Another set of players are the many prominent environmental groups, such as the Sierra Club, that have come to recognize the importance of stressing job quality policy when advocating for new clean energy policy.

A good summary of the situation with respect to advocacy organizations was provided by Emerald Cities in a memo circulated to the presidential transition team shortly after the 2008 election:

> The cooperation problem is that almost all potential members of this public, who in fact have broad agreement on emerald ends, have different "first" interests in acting on them. Labor first wants job standards and new members, community groups first want economic opportunity and respect, business first wants a return on its capital, environmentalists first want progress repairing nature, and so on. These first interests are often in conflict, stalling progress in achieving the bigger end, and often making them worse off individually, not just as a group.[6]

Perhaps surprisingly, employers have not been very prominent actors in the debates and political maneuvering around these new weatherization jobs. One reason is that at the national level, representatives of the very large non-union residential sector regard the WAP program as small relative to the size of the industry and not worth the trouble, given the role the federal government plays in imposing Davis-Bacon wage requirements on the work. As a leader of the National Association of Homebuilders commented to us:

> Most of our guys have fewer than ten employees and don't have the sort of administrative backup to handle compliance with the Davis-Bacon requirements—regardless of the wage issue. [They] kind of threw up their hands and

said, "It's not even worth trying for us to get into it, because we're kind of locked out of the system anyway because there are entities who have already existed to gather that money up and now they've layered on the Davis-Bacon requirements.

At the local level it is certainly the case that many small remodelers and construction companies have an interest in the work, but they are not organized to be actors in the local political scene and hence have had no noticeable impact. The only important exceptions are the newly founded environmentally oriented firms in several cities that have emerged as players in the debate. Like the community action agencies, these contractors express concern about a trade-off between the number of homes that can be weatherized and the quality of the jobs created. However, the reason for their focus on output is different. Where the community action agencies focus on the need to reduce the utility bills of the poor, these employers talk about their desire to save the environment. For example, the founder of a company based in Portland, Oregon, had the following to say about the company's mission:

Our primary goal is energy savings in an efficient and comfortable fashion. Why most of us got into this business is for the environmental benefits, to promote deep energy retrofits. We don't want that to get lost by setting requirements or doing things in a way that sacrifices that for the benefit of other social needs.

These contractors have generally positioned themselves to accommodate the interests of the other progressive constituents and by doing so have become preferred providers. They express a willingness to give new job quality standards a shot, especially if it leads to getting more business. As a result, they tend to exert what might be termed a slightly moderating influence in the job quality debate, but they do not push against it as aggressively as one might expect from other employers.

The Narrative: Washington and the Cities

At the national level, the best-known effort to set wage standards for government contracts is the Davis-Bacon Act. Passed in 1931, Davis-Bacon requires that federally funded construction projects pay prevailing wages for the community. This wage is determined by Labor Department surveys and is often set at union rates. The effect of the law is to establish a floor, often a union floor, below which wages may not fall.

The Weatherization Assistance Program had always been exempt from Davis-Bacon, but during the debate over the stimulus, House Democrats managed to insert last-minute language requiring that all programs funded by the bill be subject to Davis-Bacon. This led to considerable controversy. Community action agencies opposed Davis-Bacon on the grounds that higher wages would reduce the number of homes serviced. Surprisingly, there was also opposition within the federal government as the Department of Housing and Urban Development (HUD) sought exemptions for its own weatherization work.

Five months after the passage of the stimulus, the Department of Labor decided that Davis-Bacon would apply, but a new wage classification would be created for weatherization workers. Even then, in the words of one union leader, there was a fight over whether the prevailing wage would reflect "what currently prevails, as opposed what maybe ought to prevail. . . . The fight was eventually won by those who argued for what currently prevails." By mid-August, when the Department of Labor began releasing local wage determinations for the states, it was clear that Davis-Bacon would not be used to push up weatherization pay rates. As a union leader in Boston put it: "The prevailing wages are really not substantially different from what has been the standard practice in the industry, which is not what I would call a high-road direction." This made at least some unions reluctant to push Davis-Bacon in subsequent legislation. For example, the national union federation Change to Win did not push for the inclusion of Davis-Bacon in the Home Star bill, also known as Cash for Caulkers.

With respect to other dimensions of job quality—access to training and career ladders—the federal government was largely silent except for early boilerplate language issued by the Office of Management and Budget (OMB).[7] Although some organizations tried to insert language that would address these issues, a representative from Green for All said that these efforts were "pushed off" because legislators did not want to hold up the bill and thought that putting conditions on the money would cause delays. The only real effort to address training and job access was through a relatively small $500 million demonstration grant for green job training through the Department of Labor.

BOSTON

Boston boasts a dense network of community groups and unions as well as a long history of creative job training programs. In addition, both the state of Massachusetts and the city of Boston were well known for their efforts to address climate change long before the passage of the Recovery Act. Altogether, it seemed to us a good site to visit in order to understand how the job quality issue plays out at the local level.

Our interviews revealed a complicated picture. The range of groups working to shape the weatherization industry is impressive, and at one level they have much in common. They all profess concern about improving the quality of the work, and they all are interested in enhancing energy efficiency. The rub comes from two directions. First, some of the actors—notably unions and community groups—have a history of mistrust that is difficult to overcome. Second, while all of the groups can sign on to a general statement of goals, their actual priorities differ. Like their counterparts at the national level, some emphasize community access to the work, others focus on energy efficiency, and still others prioritize wages and working conditions.

Prior to the stimulus, the low-income weatherization program in Boston had been administered for over thirty years by Action for Boston Community Development (ABCD), the local community action agency. In 2008, ABCD's annual budget for this program was about $700,000. The program employed two auditors and about six subcontractors whose crews performed whatever work was found to be necessary on the audited homes. Wages were around $12 an hour for entry-level workers—far below the starting pay for a union laborer. The organization's primary goal had been to maximize the number of homes it served, an objective that placed a premium on low costs; raising the wages and working conditions of weatherization contractors did not seem to be a priority of the program.

Indeed, ABCD viewed job quality as a low-priority concern. As the key manager put it, "We got into this so that people could actually save money on their heating costs. If you don't do the most amount of work that you can do when you're in that house, you're not really accomplishing that task." He went on to add:

> Again, our main goal—I could care less about the contractors really—we're trying to help the clients that are low-income, help reduce their heating bills. That's why we exist, and I want the work to be high-quality, accountable, so that we know we're getting what we want them to do, which is to save 30 percent of their heating bill so the demand for fuel is less. That's really what we're all about. If we can garner some other social goals on the way, that's great.

Although the program may have been too small to organize or campaign around before the recession, local community advocates and unions took note when it was announced that ABCD's budget would increase sixfold over three years. The main group leading these efforts, the Green Justice Coalition, began organizing in late 2007, when the state was working on clean energy legislation. The coalition comprises labor, environmental, and community partners from across the state of Massachusetts. They see the energy efficiency industry as a place where less-skilled workers from low-income communities and communities of color can get jobs, while reducing the cost of utilities for low-income households and lowering carbon emissions.

Speaking about the new funding opportunities flowing from the stimulus, one advocate said, "We looked at this not just as green jobs, but how the green economy was an opportunity to rebuild our communities, to not have our communities left out of a new economy." ABCD's model of serving the poor without addressing the problems created by paying people low wages seemed hypocritical. "There's a lot of tension with our community groups and CAP [community action program] agencies in some cities."

Adding to the stew, Boston unions saw the weatherization program as a potential entrée into residential work and a source of employment for their members. Some community organizations feared that historically white craft unions would hoard the jobs for their members at the expense of people from poor and minority communities. A community activist who was sympathetic to the concerns of unions commented: "The problem is in Boston and Massachusetts and all over the country, the trades have been very bad at working with our community and specifically have a history of racism and sexism and a culture of good-old-boy networks that's a big elephant in the room." This viewpoint was repeated in conversations with other community leaders and local government officials.

A second conflict emerged among unions themselves as they vied for control of the work (and a future foothold in the unorganized residential construction industry). Consider the viewpoint of a leader of the Carpenters local who thought that his rates were being undercut by the Laborers. "We already have a structure in place and the rates are slightly higher, but that's what we think is appropriate because we want to elevate the wages, not just leave them where they are." This competition has made it easy for contractors to justify being non-union. As one commented, "In Massachusetts there's like five or six different unions competing for this work. Even if we thought it was necessary for us to partner with a union right now, it's like, why pick one right now? We don't know who's going to be the winner."

After the passage of the stimulus bill, several months of research and meetings with ABCD bore little fruit in terms of job access or job quality. Wages were established at Davis-Bacon levels, as newly required by the federal government. However, since these rates were intentionally set at going rates for weatherization workers rather than for commercial construction, the impact was modest at best. By the summer of 2009, it had become clear that ABCD was not interested in changing its model, and unions and community organizations had decided it was time to choose a different target. In the absence of external pressure, the nature of the jobs contracted through ABCD would not change.

Two other efforts in Massachusetts had somewhat greater effects on job quality. The first flowed from the Green Communities Act of 2008, which created a program dubbed Mass Save, funded by the utilities out of their rate receipts. The Green Justice Coalition set its sights on shaping the weatherization jobs created by this bill. They attempted to introduce "responsible em-

ployer language" but faced opposition from the utility companies and contractors who sat on the Energy Efficiency Advisory Council, the body
established to oversee the development of the three-year implementation
plans. One coalition member explained that those who were "involved in the
current system of delivery" were nervous about requiring more paperwork of
the small mom-and-pop contractors who did this work. They were also nervous about labor coming in and "turning this into something that essentially
will become a cost-ineffective enterprise." To avoid liability, the utilities had a
history of contracting out all of their energy efficiency programs to one firm,
which then hired subcontractors to do the physical work after a house had
been audited. This existing relationship may have also contributed to the
utilities' reluctance to include job quality standards in their three-year plans.

For their part, the unions that were members of the Green Justice Coalition were open to looking at how their standard wages could be adjusted to
work within the constraints of the weatherization industry. They were most
nervous about the job access piece of the coalition's campaign. A proposal
developed by the Green Justice Coalition included "targeted hiring and ap-
prenticeships, [but] we stopped short of putting percentages in there, which
some efforts in some other places have done, but partly that was because we
have internal conflicts over that with labor."

In October 2009, the Green Justice Coalition succeeded in adding job
quality language to the utilities' three-year plans. The language, however, was
very general and addressed only workforce development goals. In addition to
the foregoing efforts, the Green Justice Coalition proposed to work with the
utilities to improve job quality by aggregating demand. The challenge was
achieving any broad reform in working conditions in an industry dominated
by "three men and a truck" firms. The strategy was to "bundle" properties—
that is, aggregate weatherization demand from multiple households into one
large bundle that would be a large enough job to attract more substantial
contractors, who in turn would be easier to organize or to work with around
standards.

After a yearlong campaign, the utilities agreed to try five pilot projects.
The proponents believed that the utilities would be interested in bundling
because they felt pressure from state legislation to spend the system benefit
charge money at a faster pace. A leader of an advocacy group commented,
"They liked the idea of bundling because they could then go to their regulators and say, 'We're good boys and girls, and we did 150 units here and 150
units there.' So there's sort of this interesting kind of convergence of interest
coming together on these pilots." Nevertheless, as of November 2010, only
one pilot had moved beyond the planning stage. It was difficult to get high-
road contractors interested in the pilots because they did not see sufficient
profit margins. There was resistance from other players as well.

As of late 2010, nearly two years into the surge in weatherization funding, there had been very little progress in aggregating demand in a way that would permit easier union organizing, and the utilities had not set binding job quality standards for their contractors. The industry remained "three men and a truck," and as such the nature of the work had not changed.

By contrast to the frustration at the state level, the Green Justice Coalition had more success in influencing the city of Boston's effort, a program called Renew Boston. Unlike the Mass Save program, which already had an existing primary vendor and contractors, Renew Boston was started from the ground floor during the spring of 2010. Next Step Living, a Boston-based company founded in 2008, was looking for market share and knew that having a "triple bottom line" would make it more competitive in its bid to run the program. Many of the members of the Green Justice Coalition are based in Boston, and Community Labor United (CLU), one of the coalition's founding organizations, had been in discussion with the city since 2007 about how it could address "green" job quality and access. Contractors and the city knew that CLU and the Green Justice Coalition would vocally criticize any new program that did not address job quality and job access.

Next Step Living initiated a conversation with CLU and the Green Justice Coalition before the request for proposal (RFP) was released to see what goals they had in common. When Next Step Living submitted its bid, it included letters of support from CLU and the Green Justice Coalition. In the spring of 2010, the city of Boston, Next Step Living, Mass Energy Consumers Alliance, CLU, and the Green Justice Coalition negotiated a memorandum of understanding (MOU) that applied to this work.

The MOU sets goals for local contracting and hiring; hours of work performed by women, minorities, and people with criminal records; wages, health insurance, overtime pay, and proper employee classification; city support in helping contractors meet their workforce goals; and monitoring and reporting. The MOU did not address unions because, according to one advocate who is very close to the unions, "There are responsible union and non-union contractors. It's an expectation that most residential contractors are non-union." Although not required by the city (which in fact expressed ambivalence about a union role), Next Step Living offered to subcontract out 25 percent of the insulation work to union signatories.

The MOU contained no requirements for training, career ladders, or certification, and this remained a source of some controversy. CLU staff reported that they had interviewed insulation workers who received no training or health and safety protection. "They're undocumented. . . . It parallels what's happening in the residential construction industry." With respect to formal entry into union apprenticeship programs, two problems emerged. First, with so many craftspeople unemployed, unions had little incentive to admit new members and, in fact, faced internal opposition to doing so. Second, there was no clear path from a residential weatherization training program to the well-paid jobs found in public-sector and commercial construction.

PORTLAND AND HOUSTON:
CITIES AT THE TWO EXTREMES

If we array cities on a spectrum of how aggressive they have been in using the new weatherization funding to improve the quality of work, then Boston would be in the middle, Portland, Oregon, would be at the most aggressive end, and Houston, Texas, would be found at the least aggressive end. Understanding the story in these two cities puts the issues in a broader context.

In Portland, advocacy groups, employers, unions, and the city negotiated a community workforce agreement (CWA) that is widely regarded as a national model. The agreement applies to Clean Energy Works Portland, a revolving homeowner loan fund established to help finance weatherization for middle-income households. The CWA addresses wages, benefits, and job access. Wages are pegged to either 180 percent of the Oregon minimum wage or the Davis-Bacon weatherization rate, whichever is higher. This comes out to about $15 an hour as a minimum starting wage for weatherization workers, compared to the roughly $10 an hour they were making prior to the agreement. It is required that 80 percent of new hires be recruited from the local workforce, and all new weatherization employees are supposed to come from designated training programs until half of nonsupervisory hours are being performed by training program graduates. At least 30 percent of the work hours must be performed by underrepresented groups, including racial minorities, women, and low-income residents. In addition, the agreement tests the neighborhood-based bundling model (in order to achieve scale to attract high-quality contractors). An oversight committee with government and community membership has been established to monitor the agreement, and two unions have gone through the process to become certified trainers for the program. Although non-union contractors perform the majority work, they have nevertheless hired new employees from these union programs.

What were the politics that enabled Portland to achieve this agreement? The city, working with Green for All, led negotiations that included about fifty community groups, unions, and employers; about thirty ultimately signed on. The stakeholders credited both external pressure and public-sector initiative as reasons for the negotiation of the community workforce agreement. Around the time the CWA dialogue began, the Coalition for Communities of Color released a report on race and economic opportunity, and Portland was found to have more disparity than other cities on the West Coast. This put community organizations and the mayor on the same page with regard to concerns about equity. Even though the city had developed previous initiatives to expand contracting opportunities for minority- and women-owned businesses, one participant thought that the city's use of the term "equity" was "pretty landmark."

Community groups played an important role in keeping pressure on the city. The leader of Verde, one such group, said that organizations from across Portland had started getting together to talk about green jobs before Clean Energy Works Portland kicked off.

> We were already coming together at a community level in a multi-agency way to try to figure out how are we going to get some green jobs for our communities, and so there was. It wasn't as mature as it is now, but there was an existing capacity across community-based organizations—Latino community, Native community, black community, Asia–Pacific Islander community, pre-apprenticeship programs—that we already started trying to figure this stuff out.

Although there had been some history of union and community tension, much as in other cities, it was also true that the Laborers Union had long been a member of a broad-based community organization and had gotten to know some other community organizations through their involvement. Another community leader, speaking of the unions, commented, "I think they've been very strong in this process in terms of supporting things that really don't have anything to do with their direct benefit." For example, unions supported setting goals for minority business participation, which "doesn't necessarily mean more or less union members."

Contractors also came aboard during the negotiation process. They were active in negotiating hiring requirements and wages and were able to push back on some ideas, such as one that would have required 100 percent of their crew to be locally sourced. In the end, they were satisfied with the agreement. Their main worry was that the program would become too bureaucratic, as one contractor made clear:

> I wanted to make sure that it was fair, that it was workable, that it was not going to turn us into being another heavily weighted government-type program with a lot of regulation and things that are not normally approachable by small contractors. That it would still make sense. . . . You know we're one of the larger organizations in Portland, so some of these companies are much smaller. Just a few people at this point.

Finally, the role of political leadership in Portland was crucial. When asked why the city chose to make job quality an issue, a representative of Green for All explained:

> The project was the mayor's vision, and he wanted it to be a model project. He also wanted to do the right thing by community groups and labor. So in the

spring the city started holding roundtable discussions by sector to see how standards could be brought into the legislation. In the late summer they decided to do a more formal process, with Green for All as the facilitator.

In contrast to Portland, the story in Houston is short and simple, if not sweet. Since 2005, the city's Residential Energy Efficiency Program had been using a model similar to bundling to weatherize homes in lower-income neighborhoods. From 2006 until 2009, four larger contractors performed about $6.9 million worth of work on seven thousand homes in the area. While different from the models in Portland and Boston in that it did not involve contracting with community organizations to do outreach to residents, Houston's program was designed in a way that would seem ideal for organizing around job quality and job access. Nevertheless, the AFL-CIO union regional organization reported to us that they were unaware of any union organizing around residential work and that they did not get involved in weatherization. In commenting on its relationship with city government regarding hiring and career ladder concerns, the director of the leading community training organization said, "I am trying, but there seems to be this hands-off, like, 'Well, they're contractors, we can't control who they hire.' That kind of not wanting to intervene on that level."

Making Progress on Improving Job Quality

What do these stories tell us about the politics of job quality? At first glance, the outcomes are not very encouraging. Nothing happened in Houston, and the progress in Boston and even Portland was modest. The more ambitious programs put in practice were only pilots, and it is unclear how far they will expand. Throughout the country, the link to job ladders is weak and any link to union apprenticeship programs is nearly nonexistent. The channeling of stimulus funds to community groups for neighborhood-based outreach is reminiscent of the community action programs of the War on Poverty, which were in many ways simply efforts to buy off a constituency by creating a dedicated funding stream.[8]

This is a defensible reading, but one that we believe is both too pessimistic and not very helpful. The starting point is to understand that changing employment practices on a large scale takes a long time—considerably more time than most participants recognize at the beginning of the effort. The tasks of organizing advocates, moving government policymakers, and engaging the private sector are time-consuming. Subsequently, putting plans into practice itself is a major enterprise.

One important achievement is that job quality in weatherization was made salient, whereas before it was ignored. As a national community action agency representative put it:

It is now a much more important question than it used to be. It used to be primary emphasis on results, transparency, accountability, and quality on the home that was weatherized. The first thing was how you made a difference in that family's life. And everyone was paying the best that you can. Now it's at least equal. Quality of life for the family, but also knowing the federal investment in this program, and the federal priority especially in a recession, sustainable quality jobs are a much higher priority. And that's a question that we've never had to worry about, but now we do.

Evidence in support of this point is that even though the community action agencies were not directly touched by any of the initiatives we studied, they now felt compelled to talk about job quality as one of their concerns and objectives.

Second, the effort to improve the quality of weatherization jobs brought together groups that in the past had a long history of mistrust, if not outright antagonism. A representative of an advocacy organization in Boston acknowledged the rough history, but noted:

I respect that. . . . But on the other hand, there's community groups that say, "Yeah, we see unions as a good career pathway." And it's the rebuilding of our communities that's important, and us having good jobs, and having some sort of long-term plan for not these dead-end jobs, but a long-term plan for our communities. That's good because there are community groups that are willing to struggle through with some of our unions. And on the flip side there are unions that are sticking with us. . . . And it's been great. It's what builds the trust. Having people at the table saying, "It's a new day."

All this being said, a fair conclusion would have to be that when it came to shaping a new occupation and pushing it in the direction of high-quality work, considerably less progress was made than seems desirable. It simply proved to be much harder to move the needle than expected. Why was this the case, and what does it tell us about the politics of job quality?

POLITICAL LEADERSHIP IS CRUCIAL BUT HAS PROVED EQUIVOCAL

Advocates lacked the power to successfully raise the quality of jobs, and their task was made even more difficult by the somewhat divergent interests of members of their coalition. Making a real dent in job quality requires the commitment of political leadership to the issue. This commitment must include not only a willingness to establish and enforce standards but investments in training and other efforts to build job ladders that help weatherization employees move up the construction occupational hierarchy. Such political commitment was not consistently provided.

We have already seen that the federal government was unwilling to use Davis-Bacon to push wages up beyond the existing level. Nor did any of the funding streams require that weatherization workers receive significant training or that the jobs be connected to union or non-union career ladders. The only effort along this line was a modest Department of Labor demonstration program. Job quality was simply not a high federal priority when it came to weatherization.

The conclusion that flows from this is not that the federal government does not care about the issue but rather, as we have seen throughout the chapter, that job quality competes with other objectives and often gets lost in the shuffle. After all, in all fairness, federal leadership was confronting an unprecedented economic crisis and understandably was most concerned with pushing money out and putting people to work. This priority certainly reduced any willingness to impose job quality standards that might slow spending.

Nevertheless, it should also be understood that the pressure to spend cannot be the full story, since timidity with respect to job quality carries echoes of past episodes—for example, the reluctance we have documented around the minimum wage. Job quality is simply often not high on the agenda, and until that changes, it will be hard to make very much progress.

The federal attitude was reflected at the state and local levels—most obviously in the Houston case, where there was simply no political commitment to the issue whatsoever. However, even in much more progressive Massachusetts, the governmental role was shaded. For example, the state government was not a strong partner in the push for job quality. A sense of the reluctance around this at the state level can be gained from a comment by a senior staffer at the state Clean Energy Center when asked how the center prioritized job quality compared to other objectives: "It's definitely not important to us. . . . I don't think we want to be supporting jobs that don't give sustainable wages to people. But we don't dictate that either. We want to train people, and energy savings is the metric. I don't care who's doing it as long as it's done well and we're getting results out of that."

In Boston, the mayor's office was also reluctant to push hard on wages for the Renew Boston initiative. There was debate during the MOU negotiations over wage rates. Community Labor United and some of its partners wanted wages to be set higher than the Davis-Bacon prevailing wage for weatherization workers. The city was prepared to side with the contractor and oppose this because, "for one thing, it would make it a lot more difficult to meet the greenhouse gas reduction goals [that is, fewer units would get done]," said one city official. This official raised other issues with paying a higher wage:

If you're requiring very high wages, it's actually harder for minority and women-owned start-up entrepreneur companies to get into the business, because you're cutting their profit margins and they have to pay their employees more and it makes it harder for them. That's one issue. The other issue is that the higher the wages are, the less number of jobs there are. So that's kind of a trade-off too.

Why was Portland able to push further on job quality than either Boston or Houston? It seems clear that the answer lies in the role of government. Portland benefited from having a strong mayor who was committed to the issue and from the efforts of advocacy groups that had a good history of working together as well as political power.

Conclusion

The efforts recounted here to improve weatherization jobs show the complexity of moving forward on job quality. Improving the quality of work is a goal that competes against other legitimate and important objectives—in this case, maximizing the number of homes that are weatherized, finding employment for unemployed construction craft workers, and simply spending stimulus money as rapidly as possible. But we cannot ignore history. When it comes to job quality, political reluctance has been a long-standing theme, and the slow progress on improving the quality of weatherization jobs cannot be entirely attributed to the particulars of this case.

It seems clear that to make substantial progress the government must play a key role in pushing up job quality. Advocacy groups do not have enough leverage on their own to get the attention of the private sector, much less to shift private-sector employment practices. Only government, through its power to regulate and enforce, can do this. This was apparent in Boston and Portland, where city and state government policies were crucial, and it is even more apparent at the federal level given the key role that both Davis-Bacon and subsequent wage determinations played regarding stimulus-funded projects.

That being said, the role played by government in this story points to a very mixed conclusion. The experience with Davis-Bacon, which simply ratifies the status quo, suggests that even with a Democratic administration and a Democratic Congress there was considerable reluctance to move aggressively on job quality. Even the city of Boston was reluctant to press for higher wages. Part of the problem was the push-back against strong standards from putative allies—the local community action agencies and some federal departments, such as HUD. In addition, the unions, with the partial exception of the Laborers and the Carpenters, did not feel that they had much at stake because they had already largely abandoned residential construction. Also, in an industry so decentralized and structured around small contractors, there was a reasonable reluctance to swoop in and impose a much higher wage floor.

This is important because in the end, progress on a significant scale will require finding a way to organize the market more broadly. Small initiatives with best-practice firms are not enough because the larger market, and the forces of supply and demand it generates, will keep job quality low unless checked. As things stand, there is no real way for private actors to get their arms around the market for weatherization and achieve a broad reform. The market is too decentralized, and unions cannot play the role they do in commercial construction because their reach is very limited in residential construction. At this point only government can do the job. But as a consequence of political reluctance, forward steps are limited to experimentation and pilot programs, which have a very limited and fragile impact on the nature of weatherization work overall.

CHAPTER 9

Conclusion

One-quarter of working adults find themselves in jobs that pay wages that hover at the poverty level, and their prospects for climbing into higher-paid work are daunting. The myth of upward mobility is just that for these people—a myth. These grim economic circumstances hurt families and communities and damage our political culture. Because many other Americans are at risk of falling into the low-wage labor market, the problem is even broader than it may seem.

This book addresses this challenge. At the core of the book are several interrelated points: First, we must go beyond the view that the only action worth taking is to improve the education and skill levels of the workforce. Such improvement is important, but it is not enough. Second, we must work directly with firms to improve job quality. Third, if we are willing to take this step, then there are policies and initiatives that hold considerable promise. Finally, we must overcome aversion to government and recognize that thoughtful public policy is essential for progress.

To develop these arguments, we began by refuting myths that block action. We showed that education is important but not the master solution; that mobility out of the low-wage labor market is slow to nonexistent for adults; that full employment alone is not the solution; that we cannot blame the persistence of low-wage jobs on immigration; and that international evidence as well as research on homegrown policies such as the minimum wage show that it is possible to improve labor market conditions for those at the bottom without adversely affecting economic growth.

We stress the central importance of working with firms to improve the quality of the work they offer. Although we certainly agree that the education and skill levels of the workforce need to be improved, the fact is that to effectively improve the quality of work we have to upgrade the quality of the jobs that will never go away: the hotel room cleaners and the unskilled construction laborers and the hospital orderlies and the myriad other low-paid workers.

We believe that the problems in the low-wage labor market by and large do not flow from greedy lawbreaking employers but rather from the realities of the economic and competitive situation that firms face. There are, of course, violations of employment standards, but even these should generally be considered the result of the circumstances that firms confront as they try to make their way in a very difficult environment. Viewing firms as "the enemy" does not offer a promising way forward. We propose a strategy that relies on carrots and sticks—or to use a more sophisticated framing, beneficial constraints. Firms should be pushed to improve job quality; when they do so, they will find themselves rewarded by improved productivity flowing from higher levels of commitment and effort by their workforce as well as lower rates of turnover. The encouragement will come from an improved regulatory regime and from employee voice and community organizations. The support will come from public assistance in training their workforces and upgrading their employment practices, as well as from a regulatory policy that rewards good behavior.

The idea of both pushing and assisting is based on the observation that for a variety of reasons—competitive pressure, limited managerial resources, lack of information—firms frequently do not organize themselves in the optimum manner. If pushed, for example, through enhanced employment standards to improve their employment practices, they may well find that there are gains to be had from this strategy that had been either unrecognized or unattainable before. Assistance to firms, in the form of training subsidies or aid in creating new career paths, can play an important role in this transition.

Many—in fact most—of the steps we advocate have been implemented in bits and pieces throughout the country, and others have been proposed by a wide range of scholars and policy activists. In discussing these, we have tried to be realistic about what works well and what does not, but we have also tried to offer a unified framework, a way of thinking about the policies as a whole.

All this being said, it is also true that from the firm's perspective the gains from high-road employment practices are uncertain and taking the path in that direction is very risky in terms of competitive position and survival. And it must be recognized that, for at least some firms, the gains do not offset the costs. For both of these reasons, active policy is important to assist firms that wish to upgrade their employment practices and to push other firms in that direction.

Securing Progress

In today's economy, the pressures on firms are relentless, and the temptation is great to compete by squeezing labor—or to revert to that practice. Recall the discussion in chapter 4 of the high-road firms and high-road partnerships that have collapsed under the weight of competition.

Why is progress so fragile, and what can be done to better secure gains? There are two steps in answering this question. The first is to think of today's labor market as one whose structure and rules are in flux and to some extent up for grabs. The world of secure jobs, long-term loyalties between employers and employees, and sharing of productivity gains among all parties is gone and unlikely to return. But what will take its place? A dominant best-practice model has not emerged, and it is still unclear if it will and what form it will take. A key source of uncertainty centers on employment relationships. On the one hand, the severe competitive pressure that we have documented seems to push in the direction of squeezing employees. On the other hand, the extensive evidence that a committed workforce can produce better-quality products and better customer service seems to push in the other direction. To understand this tension, think about the difference between service quality on Southwest Airlines, with its commitment to both its workforce and its customers, and service quality on any number of the legacy airlines. The same debate is being played out in numerous industries, and the outcome is still up for grabs.

In effect, a contest has been joined, or at least should be joined, between advocates of a purely marketized view and those who believe that an effective—not to mention fair—economic order requires that norms govern employment, that employees have a channel for their voice, and that the social costs and benefits of economic activity be considered. But if these choices are in fact still uncertain, and if there is a struggle over the outcome, it must also be admitted that until recently it seemed that those holding the latter view were very much on the defensive. However, it is at least possible that the Great Recession has opened up opportunities to make this case, both because the pain that it inflicted is so widespread and because the underlying sources of the crisis seem to reside in a market mentality gone out of control.

What would it take to secure a fairer labor market? To increase the chances that agreements such as the San Francisco Hotel Partnership could survive? To provide the institutional foundation that would enable firms to provide better jobs? These are very difficult questions because pressures on firms are so great that, as we have just seen, even well-intentioned high-road efforts frequently fail. The implication would seem to be that the answer cannot lie entirely in employer practices and strategies but rather that what is needed is a broader political, social, and economic environment that supports progressive employment strategies.

The Essential Role of Public Policy

Throughout this book we have described, in what we hope are convincing terms, what can be accomplished by private actors. The actions of unions, business associations, and community groups as they all work hard to improve job quality are all important and help move us forward. But at the end of the day it seems clear that we will not accomplish what needs to be done without the active involvement of government—particularly the federal government. In this era in which government is seen as the problem, we want to argue that in fact it is an essential element in any solution. The narrative developed in the last chapter on green jobs emphasized this point: progress has been slow in improving job quality in this emergent occupation largely because of the hesitant policies of the federal government and some local governments. Without creative public policy, we are unlikely to make adequate progress.

One challenge to thinking about public policy is what might be called the long-standing "master-myth" that government has no place in regulating the economy, that if the invisible hand is left unimpeded we will all be better off. Distrust of government is a venerable theme in American history and reappears on a regular basis to discredit public policy. But this myth, at least in its most general form, is not in much need of demolishing these days. It is generally agreed that the financial markets collapsed in large measure because the government failed to provide adequate regulation and that this in turn led to the worst economic downturn since the Great Depression. No one today would seriously argue that government should leave the private economy to self-regulate. Polling supports this conclusion: according to national polls undertaken by the widely respected and nonpartisan Pew Research Center, a majority of Americans believe that government regulation of business is necessary to protect the public interest, while only 38 percent believe that government regulation generally does more harm than good.[1]

There is, however, another version of the antigovernment narrative: public policy might make sense when it comes to financial markets or food safety, but any efforts to raise standards in the job market will kill jobs. As we argue momentarily, regulation needs to be smart and sensible, and certainly some complaints are valid. But the instinctive claim that employment standards kill jobs seems reflexive and has been refuted for a century. In 1914, after the tragic Triangle Shirtwaist Factory fire, the head of the Manufacturers Association opposed any standards by saying, "We have been legislated to death," and this erroneous refrain has been echoed throughout the years.[2] That standards inevitably kill jobs is a myth, as we showed when we discussed the job creation record of other developed nations that have matched or exceeded our success while raising standards in the labor market, and as we also showed when we described research on the minimum wage that demonstrates that it does not cost employment. Of course, bad or thoughtless standard-setting can indeed have negative consequences, and later in this chapter we discuss how to avoid this trap. But first, what are the elements of an effective policy?

First Do No Harm

Doctors are taught the rule "First do no harm" early in their education, and the same wisdom is relevant to government. We saw in chapter 5 that federal, state, and local governments increasingly contract out for services, and there is considerable evidence that many of these jobs fall below our standards for decent work. In addition, a great deal of private-sector employment in low-wage jobs—the health industry being the best example—is funded by taxpayers. Public-sector leadership in improving job quality would directly upgrade the circumstances of millions of people and also help change normative expectations throughout the labor market. As we showed in chapter 1, public leadership played a central role in upgrading job quality in the twentieth century via civil service reform and regularization of personnel rules, both of which set important and influential examples for the private sector. We are now at a point where government can once again set an example.

Establishing and Enforcing Standards

In chapter 5, we discussed standard-setting at length and showed that compliance is a challenge both because of the extent of violations and because of the inherently limited resources of enforcement authorities. Nonetheless, there are a number of promising strategies for moving forward, and we described these in some detail. We also made an essential point: support for minimum standards is widespread among the American public, and regulation need not always be a burden on firms. Standards that are predictable and consistently enforced work well and are not opposed by the vast majority of employers. Indeed, there is good evidence that responsible firms support standards because they create a predictable environment and set the stage for competition based on innovation and quality rather than driving down wages.[3]

Having said all of this, it is also important to emphasize that standard setting should be sensitive to legitimate concerns regarding sometimes unreasonable burdens and unpredictable requirements. Although these complaints are sometimes self-serving efforts to kill standard-setting, they are also sometimes correct, and it does not help to pretend otherwise. This consideration leads us to a more sophisticated understanding of the role of standard-setting. The real goal is to create an environment, sometimes coercive but more often normative and supportive, that over time can shift the decisions that employers make in the direction of higher-quality work. In thinking about this, it is important to understand that such an environment would be regarded as reasonable by many employers because it does not favor one over another and it does not depend on unpredictable judgments by regulators.

SUPPORTING EFFECTIVE PROGRAMS

Incorrect perceptions to the contrary, we showed that there are effective models for working with firms to help them provide more training to their low-wage workforce and create career pathways for these employees. Despite this track record, public funding has steadily declined, leaving it to foundations to partially pick up the slack. Improved support for effective assistance to firms and employees would play an important role in enabling low-wage employers to upgrade job quality.

ESTABLISHING A SUPPORTIVE CONTEXT

Public policy establishes the context within which firms make decisions about job quality and can also strengthen the capacity of advocates for upgrading work. Health care reform enables firms to reduce the extent to which they compete on wages, while labor law reform improves the prospects for employee voice.

In addition to legislation, creative public policy can help build and establish norms in the job market. A popular image of the labor market is that it is like the market for any other commodity: buyers and sellers engage in arm's-length transactions, with each party trying to maximize their selfish interest. In this picture there is no role for social relationships, norms, or governing institutions other than the laws established by public authorities. This image is a myth even for product markets, such as finance, where it might be most expected to be true, but it certainly is a fantasy in the job market.[4] A very long-standing research tradition shows that even in what appears to be purely bourse labor markets, social structure is important in shaping outcomes: employers' associations play a role in establishing norms for jobs, intermediaries—public and private—help workers find jobs, and workers in some occupations join guilds or professional associations or unions to help them attain skills and obtain information and learn the going expectations about the terms of employment. These institutional supports play two important functions: they help the particular labor markets operate more efficiently in terms of skill acquisition and information diffusion, and in some cases they provide the scale by aggregating small jobs into groupings that can be more efficiently managed. These institutions also help establish expectations and norms about employment arrangements, and then they help diffuse these expectations in the relevant labor market.

One way of thinking about what ails the low-wage labor market is that it is disorganized and has too little structure. This observation implies that a policy goal should be to provide more effective governance in that labor market, particularly for smaller employers. We showed that the "small-firm problem" is not as intractable as it might seem: it is possible to make considerable progress through business associations and with the right attitude on the part of regulatory authorities. In one of the examples discussed in chapter 6, the Restaurant Opportunities Center's collaboration with an association of high-road restaurants in New York City has led to a manual on employment standards, cooperation with the city in issuing it, and pressure on other eateries to comply with these standards. Public policy can help build such relationships, strengthen responsible employers' associations, and lead by example by insisting that its own jobs and contractors offer decent work.

The Core Dilemma

In the name of the consumer, must we accept low wages in order to obtain low prices? Should we give in to the intense competitive pressures that drive down job quality? These are difficult and serious questions and need to be directly confronted.

Perhaps surprisingly, there is a long American tradition of debating these very issues and ample precedent for action. In the realm of political and legal theory, the choices have been characterized in different ways. The political philosopher Michael Sandel contrasts two visions of democracy: a "republican democracy" and a "procedural democracy."[5] Legal scholar James Whitman distinguishes between "consumerist" and "producerist" traditions of law.[6] Both distinctions raise the question of whether the overriding goal of the political and economic system is to maximize the well-being of consumers by freeing firms to drive prices to the lowest level or whether the goal is to achieve another objective that is in partial conflict with the consumerist vision. In Sandel's formulation, the competing objective is to enable citizens to fully participate in democratic deliberation. People who are economically marginalized, either by low wages or by reliance on public transfer payments, cannot be full citizens. In Whitman's formulation, the alternative to consumerism is to recognize that producers—firms and workers—also have rights that merit protection from the corrosive impact of competition. The anticonsumerist vision has a long pedigree of advocacy by quintessentially American leaders and scholars, such as Woodrow Wilson, Louis Brandeis, and, in some incarnations, Franklin Delano Roosevelt. It found practical expression in the anti–chain store legislation of the late 1920s and the National Industrial Recovery Act of the New Deal. Court decisions and the power of market rhetoric—and perhaps the consumer benefits of unfettered markets—seem to have defeated republican and producerist visions, but it must also be recognized that these debates move in cycles, and it is not beyond the realm of possibility that we are entering another phase.

If such a debate is possible, what does it mean in practical terms? And how might we operationalize the issue? A good way to think about these questions is to return to Wal-Mart, the poster child of low-wage work. Although by no means a typical low-wage employer, the retailer's size if nothing else makes it special, and its uniqueness has generated a research base that enables us to gauge at least roughly what is at stake. The tension that Wal-Mart raises is the trade-off of low-quality employment versus low prices—exactly the issue at hand.

As we have seen, the Wal-Mart management system pressures store managers to violate the law with respect to overtime. This is true and troubling, but it nonetheless misses the important point. Wal-Mart could clean up its practices—and there is some reason to believe that it is working to do so—but it would still be a low-wage employer. Average wages for full-time hourly workers (stockers, cashiers, and the like) are under $12 an hour, and starting wages are several dollars per hour lower. Earlier in the book, we also presented strong evidence that Wal-Mart drives down wages for employees in other retail-sector firms.

The impact of low wages is quite clear. As we have seen, low family income affects families in numerous ways. Health status worsens, education attainment falls, and children's futures dim. For adults—and the vast majority of Wal-Mart employees are adults—the chances for upward mobility are low. Wal-Mart proudly notes that many store managers started as hourly workers, but the shape of the pyramid makes it clear that for any given hourly employee the chances of such a happy outcome are vanishingly low.

There is, however, another side to the story. The evidence is also clear that prices at Wal-Mart are lower than elsewhere and that these low prices disproportionately benefit families in difficult economic circumstances. Although the exact numbers are controversial, a recent review concluded that food prices at Wal-Mart are between 8 and 27 percent lower than at large supermarket chains, and there is every reason to think that Wal-Mart prices are generally lower for other goods in addition to food.[7] Families at the lower end of the income distribution pour into Wal-Mart stores in search of these low prices.

So here we are: Wal-Mart's employment policy not only creates low-quality work for its own employees but also drives down job quality elsewhere in the labor market. Competition has consequences that we deplore. But the very same competition delivers low prices. Is there any way out of this dilemma short of acceding to the ideology of competition and consumerism or advocating for restrictions and cartels? The stakes are high because the resolution will have important consequences for the sustainability of any effort to create a more equitable job market.

In our view, the answer lies not in some abstract resolution but in everyday politics. To see this, consider what happened recently in Chicago when Wal-Mart sought to open a new store.

The history of the conflict goes back at least to 2006, when the City Council passed a big-box ordinance requiring that large stores (read Wal-Mart) pay living wages and provide health benefits. This effort was in line with many similar campaigns across the country. The ordinance passed, but the mayor vetoed it. Wal-Mart then attempted to open the new store but was met with community opposition as well as opposition from the United Food and Commercial Workers Union. However, the views of the community evolved, and in the spring of 2010 a coalition of four hundred clergy supported the store provided that Wal-Mart accepted a community benefits agreement. In the summer of 2010 the City Council ended the long fight by approving the new store.

What is the lesson here? First, it is important not to romanticize what happened. There is evidence, for example, that competing food chains have secretly financed local campaigns against new Wal-Mart stores.[8] Putting this possibility aside, however, the debate in Chicago and its resolution represent in an important way the best that we can hope for and perhaps even exactly what we do hope for: a public dialogue over the trade-off between low prices and unchecked competition, on the one hand, and decent work, on the other. Both positions have their virtues, but either position in the extreme creates an unacceptable society. The resolution to the question was compromise that acknowledges the benefits that Wal-Mart brings, but insists that its practices be moderated through the terms of the CBA. This agreement must entail some adverse price consequence (that is, higher prices), and through the political system people indicated that they would accept this. But they also indicated that they did not want to go to the other extreme and prevent Wal-Mart from doing its thing of offering cheap goods. Politics did what it is supposed to do: arrive at a solution that reflects social trade-offs. But note the key point. The social costs, the externalities, of a new Wal-Mart store—the consequences of low wages for Wal-Mart employees and their families as well as for the broader job market, which would be affected by downward pressure from Wal-Mart—were recognized, given their due weight, and not blown off as fuzzy considerations unworthy of serious consideration.

There is another lesson from Wal-Mart: countervailing power can move even the world's largest employer. Wal-Mart has come under enormous pressure regarding its employment practices and been the target of numerous lawsuits. It has had difficulty opening stores in urban areas, where it faces opposition at least partly based on its employment practices, and has often been targeted for public criticism. Perhaps surprisingly, Wal-Mart has responded to these challenges by taking steps, however halting, to upgrade the quality of the jobs it offers. The firm improved its health insurance policy and also worked with SEIU to push through the Obama health reform. It seems to have strengthened its internal controls with respect to labor law violations and has been responsive in other arenas as well, as in its efforts to reduce the negative environmental impact of its packaging. Of course, none of this is to say that Wal-Mart has shifted to the high road. Its wages are still low, and it is still a bitter opponent of any effort at worker representation. But the undeniable fact is that it has been responsive to pressure.

This leads us to the final point: the need to craft policies that have broad appeal. This point has now been made by a number of political scientists, but it has special power when applied to thinking about how to reconstruct a coalition that can undergird efforts to improve the low-wage labor market.[9] Politicians today are flocking to support programs for the middle class, and it is important to demonstrate that improving the quality of low-wage jobs is part of this agenda.

The reality is that strengthening job quality is a middle-class issue. As we saw clearly in the first chapter, in today's job market many people in decent jobs are at great risk of "falling from grace," as the sociologist Katherine Newman put it.[10] Middle-class workers faced with this risk would find it to be in their interest to have a soft landing for any such tumble. Recall the comment of one such person: "The gap between the low and middle is collapsing." Recall also the evidence that people who lose jobs take very large wage and benefit reductions if they are lucky enough to find good work. Since that next job could be in the low-wage labor market, it should also be decent, and hence improving these jobs is important to them. Indeed, even in their present jobs standards are important. Health insurance, family leave, reliable pensions, protections against discrimination based on race or gender or sexual preference—these are all broad concerns that command popular support. The agenda of improving bad jobs can be tied to these concerns. Doing so might strike some advocates as a sellout given that the needs of low-wage workers are truly more compelling than those of workers in comfortable middle-class jobs, no matter how shaky those jobs may be, but it is time to acknowledge the political reality that moving forward requires a broader political base than is currently at hand.

The importance of this point can be seen in the political history that we have recounted. Consider the story we told about efforts to raise the minimum wage under President Clinton, as well as the extended narrative in chapter 8 about green jobs. Despite strong public support, campaign promises, and control of both Houses of Congress, President Clinton hesitated for years to fight for a minimum wage increase. The narrative of green jobs also tells a tale of political timidity at both the national and local levels. The only way to overcome this political reluctance is to link the challenge of improving low-wage work to a broader set of concerns that can command a greater political audience.

The Bottom Line

We acknowledge that low wages benefit consumers, but we counter with two arguments. First, in the same cost-benefit tradition of the debate, we believe that the long-run costs of low wages have to be incorporated into the calculation. These long-run costs are real and quantifiable, and they are paid by families and communities and the body politic. But we also insist on another point: there is a moral or values argument that demands attention. In a country as rich as ours, with as great a potential as our country has, it is just unacceptable that a parent cannot attend a school conference because it would mean lost pay, that a mother ignores her diabetes because the trade-off is school books for her children, that a nursing assistant is unable to afford a safe place to live. Moral outrage does not provide a strategy for moving forward; only careful analysis can do that. But at the end of the day the moral case for creating good jobs in a wealthy nation seems to us compelling.

Chapter 1

1. Thernstrom (1964).
2. This story is told in Reddy (2011).
3. Tavernise (2011).
4. A summary of this research is in von Wachter (2011).
5. Kalleberg (2011).
6. See, for example, Jacobs and Hacker (2008). This paper reviews the earnings literature as well as the literature on family income. See also Moffitt and Gottschalk (2008).
7. Mishel (2010).
8. In 1962, the top 1 percent of households held wealth whose value was 125 times higher than that of the median household. By 1992, that figure had grown to 176 times, and in 2009, 225 times the median household's wealth. From any perspective, inequality in America is exploding. See Economic Policy Institute (2010).
9. See Osterman (1999).
10. Jencks, Perman, and Rainwater (1988); Clark (2004); Handel (2005).
11. Fremstad (2008).
12. See, for example, Blau and Kahn (2006).
13. In a nationally representative 2007 survey of firms hiring people without college degrees, researchers found that the average hourly earnings of whites was $13.08, compared to $10.23 for blacks and $11.46 for Hispanics (Acs and Loprest 2009). These earnings differences did not seem to be related to differences in education. More persuasive evidence of discrimination in low-wage jobs was found in an audit study conducted in New York City in 2004. Carefully matched and trained "applicants" responded to newspaper advertisements for jobs requiring only a high school degree. Whites received an offer or callback 31 percent of the time compared to 25 percent for Latinos and 15 percent for blacks (Pager, Western, and Bonikowski 2009).

14. Chase (2009).
15. Public Religion Research Institute (2010).
16. Cited in Waltman (2000, 65).
17. Cited in Freeman (2007).
18. These are seasonally unadjusted figures from the Bureau of Labor Statistics. The Valley numbers are for the McAllen-Eidenburg-Mission metropolitan area.
19. These figures are based on our calculations from the Current Population Survey (CPS) ongoing rotation group (ORG) data. These data and our use of them are described in more detail in the appendix.
20. DeParle and Gebeloff (2009).
21. This is based on a comparison of family budgets in the Valley to the national average family budget; see "Basic Family Budget Calculator," Economic Policy Institute, available at: http://www.epi.org/content/budget_calculator. See also "How Does Your City Stack Up?" *Kiplinger's Personal Finance*, updated May 2010, available at: http://www.kiplinger.com/tools/bestcities_sort/. This indicator of metropolitan cost of living, which puts the U.S. index at 100, has the Brownsville-Harlingen index for 2010 as 86, only 14 percent below the national average.
22. Fisher-Hoch et al. (2010).
23. A useful review of this literature is Wilkinson and Pickett (2009).
24. Sullivan and von Wachter (2009); Oreopolous, Page, and Stevens (2008); Stevens and Schaller (2009).
25. Sandel (1996), 330.
26. Jacoby (2004, 13–14).
27. The wage data that follow are taken from the ORGs (the Current Population Surveys of April and August) in which wage data are collected for that point in time. These wage data are considered to be more accurate than the wages calculated from the March CPS, which asks about earnings over the prior year and for which the wage has to be calculated by dividing annual earnings by annual hours worked, both of which are recalled with some error. The advantage of the March survey is that it also asks about health insurance and pensions, information that is not collected in the ORG data. For both the ORG data and the March survey, allocated wages are eliminated, as are wages that are reported below $1 an hour in 1979 dollars; for a discussion on processing these data, see Lemieux (2006). It is also worth noting that although in other contexts topcoding of wages is an issue, it does not affect our calculations since we focus on the median.
28. To ask about health care and pensions we must use the March CPS because the surveys we used for the discussion of wages do not ask about benefits. However, the wage data in the March surveys are less accurate than the data in the ORGs because in March wages have to be calculated by dividing respondents' reports

of total annual earnings by reported total hours worked, and there is much more room for error in reporting. In addition, the March benefits questions ask about the longest job held during the prior year, but experts believe that most people interpret the questions as being about the current job. This introduces a slight mismatch between the reporting period for wages and for benefits. We process the wage data as we do for the ORG data. In March 2007, the median is $17.60, and the percentage below our standard is 24.7 percent, both of which are very close to the ORG figures.

29. The CPS asks if the employer offers a pension plan and then asks if the respondent is included. The term "inclusion" is ambiguous, but if it is interpreted as "participation," then the decision not to participate might be driven by a variety of considerations, not just the possibility that the respondent's wages are too low to afford the deduction. And there are no questions about the availability of an employer match.

Chapter 2

1. Hertz (2006), 9.
2. Holzer (2004).
3. Theodos and Bednarzik (2006).
4. Lopreste et al. (2009).
5. Urban Institute (2006).
6. Kopczuk, Saez, and Song (2010).
7. Sawhill and Morton (2007).
8. For an excellent account of these debates, see Weir (1992).
9. Holzer, Raphael, and Stoll (2006).
10. Duncan and Trejo (2008).
11. The poverty rate for natives (of all ages) in 1994 was 13.8 percent, and in 2009 it was 13.7 percent. For foreign-born noncitizens, it was 28.5 percent and 25.1 percent, respectively. For people between the ages of eighteen and sixty-four, the poverty rates in those two years for white non-Hispanics were 8.2 percent and 9.3 percent, for blacks 23.4 percent and 21.9 percent, and for Hispanics 24.8 percent and 21.4 percent. Trends in poverty rates for natives and for non-Hispanics did not seem to be affected by the growth of immigration. See U.S. Bureau of the Census, "Historical Poverty Tables—People," available at: http://www.census.gov/hhes/www/poverty/data/historical/people.html.
12. Congressional Budget Office (2006, 22–23).
13. David Card (2009, 19) writes: "Overall, I conclude that immigration has not had much effect on native wage inequality in the U.S. as a whole. Nevertheless, because immigrants are clustered at the high and low ends of the education distribution, and because they also tend to have higher residual inequality than natives . . . wage inequality over all workers in the economy is higher than it

would be in the absence of immigration. . . . The effect is relatively small, however. . . . The presence of immigration can account for a relatively small share (4–6%) of the rise in inequality in the past 25 or so years."

14. Ottaviano and Peri (2006).
15. Borjas (2006).
16. Passel and Cohen (2009).
17. Kochhar (2010).
18. Bernhardt et al. (2009).
19. Passel and Cohen (2009).
20. Using standardized measures, we find that the U.S. poverty rate is easily the highest, at 17 percent. By comparison, France's rate is 7.23 percent, Germany's 8.3 percent, and the United Kingdom's 12.4 percent. Our poverty rate is even higher than the rates of the southern nations of Italy and Spain (see Burtless and Smeeding 2007). The data are for the early 2000s, and poverty is defined as income below 50 percent of the median.
21. Devorye and Freeman (2001).
22. Gautié and Schmitt (2010).
23. Freeman (2005a), 12.
24. The evidence on price increases is that a 10 percent hike in the minimum wage leads to a onetime increase in restaurant prices of well under 1 percent (Aaronson 2001).
25. The standard estimate among those holding to the view that employment is reduced is that a 10 percent increase in the minimum wage reduces employment by 1 percent (Brown 1999).
26. DiNardo, Fortin, and Lemieux (1996).
27. David Autor, Alan Manning, and Christopher Smith (2010, 32) write (referring to the 50/10 differential), "We estimate that 35–55% of the growth of lower tail inequality in the female wage distribution between 1979 and 1988, 35% to 45% of the growth of pooled gender inequality, and approximately 15% of the growth of male inequality—as measured by the differential between the log of the 50th and 10th percentiles—is attributable to the decline in the real value of the minimum wage."
28. Card and Krueger (1995).
29. Dube, Lester, and Reich (2010).
30. The final explanation is that firms enjoy some degree of monopsony power. The story goes as follows: in standard theory, firms gain no benefit from raising wages above market levels because they can attract all the workers they need at the going rate. However, if a firm is a dominant employer in an area, or if workers face search costs and hence do not respond to small wage increases, then a wage increase would attract more applicants. However, if firms were to raise wages for a new hire, they would have to raise the wage for all of the incumbent workers, and so they end up "under-hiring." In effect, there are vacancies here since firms would like to hire additional workers, but won't do it. A

minimum wage can increase employment when employers, faced with a forced increase in the wage, decide that they might as well hire more workers to get that extra productivity.

31. The evidence that this is true comes from findings in the Card and Krueger research that have received less attention than their work on employment impacts but that are in many ways more important. First, wage gains from the minimum wage rippled up the wage structure so that employees who were already above the new minimum, but still close to it, also received pay raises. Second, and even more strikingly, after an increase in the minimum wage, the distribution of other wages shifted: wages that were previously dispersed converged on the new minimum. This does not make sense in terms of economic theory, since people are supposed to be paid their marginal product and many of the people who were below the minimum wage should have been fired, but they were not. In addition, the spike occurred even in firms in sectors not covered by the minimum wage (or in firms too small to be covered by the minimum wage). These patterns point to the important role that the minimum wage plays in anchoring expectations and norms in the job market.

32. See Osterman (2002) for a discussion of how living wages affected the policies of community development authorities in Texas.

Chapter 3

1. As quotaed in Waldron, Roberts, and Reamer 2004, 215.
2. Waldron, Roberts, and Reamer (2004), 16.
3. Goldin and Katz (2008, 96).
4. A useful review of this literature can be found in Hilton (2008).
5. We know that within the college-educated population, the greatest gain in the past two decades has been at the very top; see Kopczuk, Saez, and Song (2010). So there is a lot of residual inequality (a wide distribution) within the college group, and the average is raised by those at the very top (most hedge fund managers have a college degree). But it is not college per se that is driving this. See also Lemieux (2006).
6. Bowles, Gintis, and Osborne (2001).
7. Cappelli (1992).
8. Duncan and Dunifon (1998).
9. This research by Melissa Osborne is described in Bowles, Gintis, and Osborne (2001, 1164–65).
10. See Andersson, Holzer, and Lane (2005). In addition, John Abowd, John Haltiwanger, and Julia Lane (2008, 81–100) show that 50 percent of the variation in earnings of workers is due to human capital and 50 percent is due to firm effects. Earlier research making the same point includes Groshen (1991).
11. Krueger and Summers (1988).
12. Acemoglu (2002).

13. Krueger and Lindahl (2001).
14. Hanushek and Woessmann (2008).
15. For a discussion of the technology story, see Autor, Levy, and Murnane (2003). For an application of this story in explaining recent trends in wages, see Autor, Katz, and Kearney (2008). See also Autor (2010).
16. Holzer and Lerman (2009).
17. Lacey and Wright (2009).
18. Kain and Rouse (1995); see also Marcotte et al. (2005). Marcotte and his colleagues estimate year 2000 wages for students who were in the eighth grade in 1988 and no longer in school when the earnings data were collected. Because the data source—the National Educational Longitudinal Survey—is quite rich, these authors were able to control for high school performance as well as a wide range of parental characteristics. These controls substantially reduce concerns regarding selection bias in driving the results.
19. Congressional Budget Office (2006, 3).
20. See Card and DiNardo (2002). They show that the vast majority of the increase in the 90/10 wage gap occurred in the early 1980s and was a onetime episodic event. "We suspect," they write, "that trends in the minimum wage, and other factors such as declining unionization and the reallocation of labor induced by the 1982 recession, can explain much of the rise in overall wage inequality in the early 1980s" (775). In another review of the evidence, Daron Acemoglu (2002, 13) writes that pure technology stories "do not provide a natural explanation for the fall in the wages of low-skill workers" and goes on to observe that more institutional explanations are needed. Finally, even strong proponents of the skill-based explanation for inequality concede that the collapsing fortunes of those in the lower tail of the income distribution that occurred in the 1980s had a great deal to do with the falling value of the minimum wage; see Autor, Katz, and Kearney (2008).

Chapter 4

1. This account is based on Leonard and Watson (2006).
2. Bernhardt et al. (2009).
3. See Andersson, Holzer, and Lane (2005); see also Abowd, Haltiwanger, and Lane (2008); Krueger and Summers (1988).
4. Eaton (1996).
5. See, for example, Mayfield (2010).
6. Cascio (2006).
7. Council of Economic Advisers (2007, table B.1).
8. Brown, Hamilton, and Medoff (1990, 20, 23).
9. Neumark, Wall, and Zhang (2011).
10. Dube, Lester, and Eidlin (2007).
11. Neumark, Zhang, and Ciccarella (2005).

12. Hausman and Leibtag (2007).
13. Carré and Tilly (2008).
14. Weil (2010a).
15. McKinsey Global Institute (2001).
16. Hoovers, "Industry Profiles: Hospitals," available at http://premium.hoovers.com.libproxy.mit.edu/subscribe/ind/fr/profile/basic.xhtml?ID=60.
17. American Hospital Association (2005).
18. Hoovers, "Industry Profiles: Hospitals," available at http://premium.hoovers.com.libproxy.mit.edu/subscribe/ind/fr/profile/basic.xhtml?ID=60.
19. Kurt Grote, Edward Levine, and Paul Mango (2006) write: "When hospitals become more focused and their patients more value conscious, they will start to resemble companies in other competitive service industries. Like cutting-edge retailers, they must identify the characteristics of the patients they can best serve and attract those people by creating specific value propositions. . . . Hospitals with weak skills and systems for extending credit or making collections at the point of service may have higher bad debts."
20. Korshak (2000).
21. Korshak (2000).
22. Gardner (2007).
23. Gautié and Schmitt (2010).
24. Gautié and Schmitt (2010, 255).
25. Gautié and Schmitt (2010, 270).
26. In 2010, Wal-Mart settled a suit in California regarding unpaid vacation time and wages for over 200,000 employees ("Discount Giant Settles Suit with California Workers," *Wall Street Journal*, May 13, 2010). In 2007, Wal-Mart settled a separate suit with the U.S. Department of Labor, again over its failure to pay for overtime ("Wal-Mart Settles U.S. Suit About Overtime," *New York Times*, January 26, 2007). In 2009, a similar settlement was reached for 87,000 Massachusetts workers ("Wal-Mart Will Pay $40 million to Workers," *Boston Globe*, December 3, 2009), and in the biggest case of all, also in 2009, Wal-Mart agreed to pay over $600 million to settle seventy-six federal and state overtime suits ("The Wal-Mart Settlement: A Preemptive Strike Against Unionization," *Wall Street Journal*, December 24, 2008).
27. Kochan (2009, 15).
28. See Brennan Center for Justice (2006, 2)
29. Interfaith Workers Justice (2008).
30. Ruckelshaus (2008).
31. Bernhardt et al. (2009).
32. In a 2006 survey of 286 domestic workers in Maryland, 75 percent did not receive overtime pay (as required by Maryland law) and about half earned less than the state minimum wage; several surveys of day laborers found widespread abuses—for example, 58 percent had been denied their wages at least once. See CASA of Maryland (2007).

33. Harris (2010).
34. Planmatics, Inc. (2000).
35. Interagency Task Force on Employee Misclassification (2008).
36. Greenhouse (2000) and Perez-Pena (2000), cited in Ruckelshaus and Gold-stein (2002).
37. See Ruckelshaus (2009).
38. Thomas (2010).
39. Dey, Houseman, and Polivka (2009).
40. Dube and Kaplan (2010).
41. Dube and Kaplan (2010, 300).
42. Reich, Hall, and Jacobs (2005).
43. Dey, Houseman, and Polivka (2009).
44. Erickcek, Houseman, and Kalleberg (2003, 395–96).
45. Whiting (2005).
46. Nelson and Winter (1982); Arthur (1994); Scott (1998).
47. Womack, Jones, and Roos (2007).
48. This idea was originated and elaborated by Wolfgang Streeck (1997).
49. Bloom and van Reenen (2010).
50. Howes (2005).
51. Seavey (2004).
52. Hinkin and Tracey (2000).
53. Reich, Hall, and Jacobs (2005).
54. Kochan et al. (2009, 226).
55. Kochan et al. (2009, 80).
56. Batt, Colvin, and Keefe (2002).
57. Koys (2001).

Chapter 5

1. Weil (2010b, 7).
2. Weil (2010b, 6).
3. Between 1975 and 2004, the number of U.S. Department of Labor (DOL) workplace inspectors declined by 14 percent and the number of compliance actions declined by 36 percent, while during the same period the number of covered employees in the labor force grew by 55 percent and the number of covered establishments grew by 112 percent (Ruckelshaus 2008, 376). In 2004, there were only 788 DOL inspectors nationwide. Real spending in 1984 dollars for federal enforcement of occupational health and safety laws, the Fair Labor Standards Act, and mining safety standards went from $284 million in 1998 to only $292 million in 2007, during which time over 1 million new workplaces were created (Weill 2010b, 5).
4. DeCarlo and Schiller (2010).
5. For example, the inspectors in Pennsylvania are responsible for minimum

wages, child labor law, overtime, wage payment and collection law, prevailing wage, farm labor, underground utility line protection, apprenticeship and training, equal pay, industrial homework, the medical fee act, and engineering testing and inspection services (DeCarlo and Schiller 2010).

6. The report quotes the *Los Angeles Times*: "According to the California Department of Industrial Relations, the number of wage and hour inspectors rose about 7% since 1980 while the state population grew 62%" (Marc Lifsher and Alana Semuels, "Harsher Penalties Suggested for Employers Who Shortchange Workers in California," *Los Angeles Times*, September 16, 2010).

7. Kutz (2008).

8. Lasowski (2008).

9. Weil (2010b).

10. Goldstein et al. (1999).

11. See, for example, Weil (2009).

12. Weil (2005).

13. These efforts are described in Weil (2010b).

14. These results are cited in Kazee, Lipsky, and Martin (2008).

15. Gabel et al. (2008).

16. Gabel, Whitmore, and Pickreigh (2007).

17. This account is based on Lee (2005).

18. Lipsky (1980).

19. Gray and Silbey (2010).

20. Piore and Schrank (2006).

21. Sabel, O'Rourke, and Fung (2000).

22. Locke, Qin, and Brause (2007).

23. This section draws heavily on a research memo prepared as part of this project by Andrew Weaver.

24. Simmons and Luce (2009, 101).

25. Gopinath (2005, 20).

26. Lang (2006).

27. CBAs were primarily identified through the community benefits agreements blog maintained by staff at the Albany Law School's Government Law Center (communitybenefits.blogspot.com). We added an additional CBA that was signed in 2011. We then searched for information on the current status of the projects from various media and government sites. If the underlying real estate project was completed as of April 14, 2011 (the target date), we categorized the relevant deal as a "completed project." Note that this status refers to the real estate deal, not the full delivery of all community benefits outlined in the CBA. In some cases, these benefits will continue for many years into the future. If the project was not completed by the target date, but available sources indicated that it had either broken ground or was clearly moving forward (securing financing, getting permits, and so on), then we categorized it as an "active project." If available sources indicated that the project was stalled or that its future

was in doubt, we categorized it as "unclear status/project in limbo." Finally, if available sources indicated that the project was no longer viable (owing, for example, to lack of financing, a change of developer plans, or the opposition of permitting authorities), we categorized the project as "defunct project." To develop the estimates of workers affected by CBAs, we began with twenty-nine CBAs. We then eliminated the three CBA projects categorized as "defunct," and we also eliminated two additional projects that were not associated with job development. One of these was the Minneapolis Digital Inclusion project, which provided Wi-Fi services and whose CBA was targeted at reducing the digital divide in Wi-Fi usage, not at job quality measures. The other was Milwaukee Park East, a CBA that involved a blanket requirement that any subsequent development on sixteen acres of county-owned land include negotiated CBAs, with the content to be determined through the negotiations. Because no development has been proposed (and there is some question about whether the county will continue to own the land), it is not possible to develop estimates of job creation.

For the twenty-four projects that remained after these adjustments, we searched for publicly available estimates of total development costs as well as estimates of the number of construction jobs and permanent jobs that the projects would create. To find these estimates, we searched for media and government reports. In the cases of completed projects or partially completed projects with updated numbers, we attempted to use actual figures or revised projections. Although actual numbers were frequently available for total development costs, in most cases there were no media or government reports assessing the actual number of jobs that a completed project had generated. In these instances, we continued to use the original projected job creation number. Thus, the data set contains a blend of projected and actual data. It is for this reason that we emphasize that this analysis is a very "back of the envelope" exercise intended to develop rough boundaries of job impacts.

To develop the lower bound of potentially impacted workers, we further restricted this subset of CBAs to only those associated with completed projects. Based on publicly available information, twelve of these CBAs are associated with completed projects (see discussion of table 5.1 methodology). Of these twelve projects, we constructed job estimates for seven projects and permanent job estimates for nine projects. If we sum the respective job totals for the projects for which we have job data, and if we make the conservative assumption that other completed projects had zero job impacts, we arrive at a total of 16,672 construction jobs and 34,841 permanent jobs. This is clearly a lower bound because it assumes both that all incomplete projects will fail to have job impacts and that the completed projects with no easily available public job estimates in fact have zero job impacts.

To develop an upper bound, we had to estimate missing job impacts for both completed and incomplete projects. We made these estimates by utilizing total development cost data. We estimated cost per job based on the data that we had, and then we divided the development costs for the projects with missing job data by the average cost per job for both construction jobs and permanent jobs. The result is estimated construction and permanent jobs for the projects with missing data.

Overall, we have total development cost data (projected or actual) for twenty-two of the twenty-four nondefunct projects. We have construction job data (projected or actual) for fifteen projects and permanent job data (projected or actual) for eighteen projects. Using these data, we calculate an average cost per job of $1,217,262 for construction jobs and $796,153 for permanent jobs. Because we have total development cost data for all relevant projects that are missing job data, we can divide the total development costs for each of these projects by the above averages to develop construction and permanent job estimates. After performing this calculation, we have estimates of job impacts for all twenty-four projects in our adjusted data set. We then sum these job impacts to arrive at an upper bound of 137,108 construction jobs and 118,074 permanent jobs. These estimates are upper bounds because it is probable that some of the twelve incomplete projects included in this data set of twenty-four projects will not come to fruition.

28. Simmons and Luce (2009).
29. Wolf-Powers (2010).
30. Edwards and Filion (2009).
31. Edwards and Filion (2009).
32. Madland and Paarlberg (2008).
33. Sonn and Gebreselassie (2009); Madland and Paarlberg (2008).
34. Freeman (2005b). As of 2005, 19 percent of living wage ordinances were in the East, 33 percent were in the Midwest, 16 percent were in the South, and 32 percent were on the West Coast.
35. The skeptical view is summarized and reviewed in Neumark and Adams (2000). The more positive view is represented in Thompson and Chapman (2006).
36. Lester (2009).
37. As an example, the Los Angeles ordinance of 1997 had a direct impact on about 6,500 people; see Fairris (2005). For a survey of the size of campaigns around the country, see Freeman (2005b).
38. Lester and Jacobs (2010).
39. Lester and Jacobs (2010).
40. Estlund (2010).

Chapter 6

1. Outgoing rotation groups, monthly Current Population Survey. These are combined data for the years 2005 to 2008 and, as throughout the book, refer

to adults. Nonmanagerial food service workers are occupational codes between 4020 and 4160; maids and housekeepers are occupational code 4230; non-managerial retail workers are occupational codes 4720, 4740, and 4760.

2. Waldinger (1998, 107).
3. Yu (2008, 144).
4. The source of the material in these paragraphs is Horwitt (1992).
5. Warren and Wood (2001).
6. See Osterman and Lautsch (1996, 1998); Rademacher, Bear, and Conway (2001); Maguire et al. (2010).
7. See Osterman (2002).
8. See Osterman (2002).
9. Fine (2006).
10. These membership rates are based on the Current Population Survey. See "Union Membership and Coverage Database from the CPS," available at: unionstats.gsu.edu.
11. The data in this section are taken from Freeman (2007).
12. See Pew Research Center (2010).
13. Ferguson (2008).
14. Ferguson (2008).
15. Schmitt and Zipperer (2009).
16. An early contribution on this point is Lipset, Trow, and Coleman (1962).
17. Yu (2008).
18. Theodore (2010).
19. Quoted in *The Economist* (2009, 52).
20. Fine, (2006, 217, 253).
21. Lichtenstein (2002, 274).

Chapter 7

1. Maguire et al. (2010).
2. Osterman and Lautsch (1996, 1998).
3. King, Smith, and Schroeder (2009).
4. This account is based on fieldwork by Elizabeth Chimienti.
5. Whiting (2005).
6. This section is based on the report by FutureWorks (2004).
7. See, for example, Pindus et al. (2004).

Chapter 8

1. *Good Jobs First* (2009, 25).
2. Conway and Gerber (2009, 7).
3. From Weatherization Assistance Program Technical Assistance Center (WAP-

TAC), "Core Competencies," chart by Bob Scott, Weatherization Director, National Association of State Community Services Programs (NASCSP).

4. Weil (2010c).
5. Biden (2009).
6. Hudson, Rogers, and Thompson (2008).
7. Section 3 of the Recovery Act states that one of the purposes of the act is "to assist those most impacted by the recession." The OMB's "Updated Implementing Guidance for the American Recovery and Reinvestment Act of 2009" expands on this by recommending that as agencies spend Recovery Act funds, they "[target] assistance consistent with other policy goals." These policy goals, which are spelled out in the memo, include ensuring compliance with equal opportunity laws and principles; promoting local hiring; providing maximum practicable opportunities for small businesses; providing equal opportunity for disadvantaged business enterprises; encouraging sound labor practices; and engaging with community-based organizations.
8. See Moynihan (1969); Piven and Cloward (1977).

Chapter 9

1. Pew Research Center (2011).
2. Baram and Stone (2011).
3. See, for example, Vogel (1995).
4. On financial markets, see, for example, Zuckerman (2004).
5. Sandel (1996).
6. Whitman (2007).
7. On Wal-Mart's food prices, see Hausman and Leibtag (2007).
8. *Wall Street Journal* (2010).
9. See, for example, Skocpol (1996).
10. Newman (1999).

REFERENCES

Aaronson, Daniel. 2001. "Price Pass-Through and the Minimum Wage." *Review of Economics and Statistics* 83(1): 158–69.

Abowd, John, John Haltiwanger, and Julia Lane. 2008. "Wage Structure and Labor Mobility in the United States." In *The Structure of Wages*, edited by Edward Lazear and Kathryn Shaw. Chicago: University of Chicago Press.

Acemoglu, Daron. 2002. "Technical Change, Inequality, and the Labor Market." *Journal of Economic Literature* 40(1): 7–72.

Acs, Gregory, and Pamela Loprest. 2009. "Job Differences by Race and Ethnicity in the Low-Skill Labor Market." Brief 4. Washington, D.C.: Urban Institute (February).

American Hospital Association. 2005. "The Fragile State of Hospital Finances." Available at: *www.aha.org/aha/content/2005/pdf/05fragilehosps.pdf*.

Andersson, Fredrik, Harry Holzer, and Julia Lane. 2005. *Moving Up or Moving On: Who Advances in the Low-Wage Labor Market*. New York: Russell Sage Foundation.

Arthur, W. Brian. 1994. *Increasing Returns and Path Dependence in the Economy*. Ann Arbor: University of Michigan Press.

Autor, David H. 2010. "The Polarization of Job Opportunities in the U.S. Labor Market: Implications for Employment and Earnings." Washington, D.C.: Center for American Progress (April).

Autor, David H., Lawrence F. Katz, and Melissa S. Kearney. 2008. "Trends in U.S. Wage Inequality: Revising the Revisionists." *Review of Economics and Statistics* 90(2): 300–23.

Autor, David H., Frank Levy, and Richard Murnane. 2003. "The Skill Content of Recent Technological Change: An Empirical Investigation." *Quarterly Journal of Economics* 118(November): 1279–1333.

Autor, David H., Alan Manning, and Christopher Smith. 2010. "The Contribution of the Minimum Wage to U.S. Wage Inequality over Three Decades: A Reassessment." Working paper. Cambridge, Mass.: Massachusetts Institute of Technology, Department of Economics (November).

Baram, Marcus, and Andrea Stone. 2011. "Triangle Shirtwaist Co. Fire's Legacy Under Threat." *HuffPostAOLNews*, March 25, 2011. Available at: http://www .huffingtonpost.com/2011/03/25/triangle-shirtwaist-co-factory-fire -legacy_n_840835.html.

Batt, Rosemary, Alex Colvin, and Jeffrey Keefe. 2002. "Employee Voice, Human Resource Practices, and Quit Rates: Evidence from the Telecommunications Industry." *Industrial and Labor Relations Review* 55(4): 573–94.

Bernhardt, Annette, Ruth Milkman, Nick Theodore, Douglas Heckathorn, Mirabaei Auer, James DeFillipis, Ana Luz Gonzalez, Victor Narro, Jason Perelshteyn, Diana Polson, and Michael Spiller. 2009. *Broken Laws, Unprotected Workers: Violations of Employment and Labor Laws in America's Cities.* New York: National Employment Law Project.

Biden, Joseph. 2009. "Green Jobs: A Pathway to a Strong Middle Class." Staff report of the Middle Class Task Force. Washington: The White House (February 27).

Blau, Francine, and Lawrence Kahn. 2006. "The U.S. Gender Pay Gap in the 1990s: Slowing Convergence." *Industrial and Labor Relations Review* 60(1): 45–66.

Bloom, Nicholas, and John van Reenen. 2010. "Why Do Management Practices Differ Across Firms and Countries?" *Journal of Economic Perspectives* 24(1): 203–24.

Borjas, George. 2006. "Wage Trends Among Disadvantaged Minorities." In *Working and Poor: How Economic and Policy Changes Are Affecting Low-Wage Workers*, edited by Rebecca Blank, Sheldon Danziger, and Robert Schoeni. New York: Russell Sage Foundation.

Bowles, Samuel, Herbert Gintis, and Melissa Osborne. 2001. "The Determinants of Earnings: A Behavioral Approach." *Journal of Economic Literature* 39(4): 1137–76.

Brennan Center for Justice. 2006. "Protecting New York's Workers." December 13. Available at: http://www.brennancenter.org/content/resource/protecting_new_ yorks_workers_full_report/.

Brown, Charles. 1999. "Minimum Wages, Employment, and the Distribution of Income." In *Handbook of Labor Economics*, edited by Orley Ashenfelter and David Card. Vol. 3. New York: Elsevier Science.

Brown, Charles, James Hamilton, and James Medoff. 1990. *Employers Large and Small.* Cambridge, Mass.: Harvard University Press.

Burtless, Gary, and Timothy Smeeding. 2007. "Poverty, Work, and Policy: The U.S. in Comparative Perspective." Testimony before the House Committee on Ways and Means, Subcommittee on Income and Family Support, February 13, 2007.

Cappelli, Peter. 1992. "Is the 'Skills Gap' Really About Attitudes?" Philadelphia: University of Pennsylvania, National Center on the Educational Quality of the Workforce.

Card, David. 2009. "Immigration and Inequality." *American Economic Review* 99(2): 1–21.

Card, David, and John DiNardo. 2002. "Skill-Biased Technological Change and Rising Wage Inequality: Problems and Puzzles." *Journal of Labor Economics* 20(4): 733–83.

Card, David, and Alan Krueger. 1995. *Myth and Measurement: The New Economics of the Minimum Wage.* Princeton, N.J.: Princeton University Press.

Carré, Françoise, and Chris Tilly, with Brandynn Holgate. 2008. "Continuity and Change in Low-Wage Work in U.S. Retail Trade." Boston: University of Massachusetts, McCormack Graduate School of Policy Studies, Center for Social Policy (April).

CASA of Maryland. 2007. "Wage Theft: How Maryland Fails to Protect the Rights of Low-Wage Workers." January. Available at: http://www.casademaryland.org/storage/documents/wagetheft.pdf.

Cascio, Wayne F. 2006. "Decency Means More Than 'Always Low Prices': A Comparison of Costco to Wal-Mart's Sam's Club." *Academy of Management Perspectives* 20(3): 26–37.

Chase, Katie Johnston. 2009. "Hundreds Attend Rally for Fired Hyatt Housekeepers; Politicians Urge Boycott of the Hotel." *Boston Globe*, September 18, 2009.

Clark, Andrew. 2004. "What Makes a Good Job? Evidence from OECD Countries." DELTA working paper 2004-28. Brussels: Centre National de la Recherche Scientifique.

Congressional Budget Office. 2006. "Changes in Low-Wage Labor Markets Between 1979 and 2005." Publication 2745 (December). Available at: www.cbo.gov/ftpdocs/76xx/doc7693/12-04-labor force.pdf.

Conway, Maureen, and Allison Gerber. 2009. "Construction Pre-Apprenticeship Programs: Results from a National Survey." Washington, D.C.: Aspen Institute (July).

Council of Economic Advisers. 2007. *Economic Report of the President.* Washington: U.S. Government Printing Office.

DeCarlo, Sarah, and Zach Schiller. 2010. "Investigating Wage Theft: A Survey of the States." Cleveland: Policy Matters Ohio (November).

DeParle, Jason, and Robert Gebeloff. 2009. "Food Stamp Use Soars Across the Country, and a Stigma Fades." *New York Times*, November 28: 25.

Devorye, Dan, and Richard Freeman. 2001. "Does Inequality in Skills Explain Inequality in Earnings Across Advanced Countries?" Working paper 8140. Cambridge, Mass.: National Bureau of Economic Research (February).

Dey, Matthew, Susan Houseman, and Anne Polivka. 2009. "What Do We Know About Contracting Out in the United States? Evidence from Household and Establishment Surveys." Working paper 09-157. Kalamazoo, Mich.: W. E. Upjohn Institute for Employment Research (September).

DiNardo, John, Nicole Fortin, and Thomas Lemieux. 1996. "Labor Market Institutions and the Distribution of Wages, 1973–1992: A Semi-Parametric Approach." *Econometrica* 64(5): 1001–44.

Dube, Arindrajit, and Ethan Kaplan. 2010. "Does Outsourcing Reduce Wages in the Low-Wage Service Occupations? Evidence from Janitors and Guards." *Industrial and Labor Relations Review* 63(2): 287–306.

Dube, Arindrajit, T. William Lester, and Barry Eidlin. 2007. "Firm Entry and Wages: The Impact of Wal-Mart Growth on Earnings Throughout the Retail Sector." Berkeley: University of California, Institute for Research on Labor and Employment.

Dube, Arindrajit, T. William Lester, and Michael Reich. 2010. "Minimum Wage Effects Across State Borders: Estimates Using Contiguous Counties." *Review of Economics and Statistics* 94(2): 945–64.

Duncan, Brian, and Stephen Trejo. 2008. "Immigration and the U.S. Labor Market." London: University College London, Department of Economics, Centre for Research and Analysis of Migration (December).

Duncan, Greg, and Rachel Dunifon. 1998. "Long-Run Effects of Motivation on Economic Success." *Social Psychological Quarterly* 61(1): 33–48.

Eaton, Susan. 1996. "Beyond 'Unloving Care': Promoting Innovation in Elder Care Through Public Policy." Cambridge, Mass.: Radcliffe Public Policy Institute.

Economic Policy Institute. 2010. "State of Working America Preview: The Rich Get Richer." Washington, D.C.: Economic Policy Institute (December 22). Available at: http://www.epi.org/economic_snapshots/entry/the_rich_get_richer/.

The Economist. 2009. "All Struck Out." October 17.

Edwards, Kathryn, and Kai Filion. 2009. "Outsourcing Poverty: Federal Contracting Pushes Down Wages and Benefits." Issues brief 250. Washington, D.C.: Economic Policy Institute (February 11).

Erickcek, George, Susan Houseman, and Arne Kalleberg. 2003. "The Effects of Temporary Services and Contracting Out on Low-Skilled Workers: Evidence from Auto Suppliers, Hospitals, and Public Schools." In *Low-Wage America: How Employers Are Reshaping Opportunity in the Workplace*, edited by Eileen Appelbaum, Annette Bernhardt, and Richard J. Murnane. New York: Russell Sage Foundation.

Estlund, Cynthia. 2010. *Regoverning the Workplace: From Self-Regulation to Co-Regulation.* New Haven, Conn.: Yale University Press.

Fairris, David. 2005. "The Impact of Living Wages on Employers: A Control Group Analysis of the Los Angeles Ordinance." *Industrial Relations* 44(1): 84–105.

Ferguson, John-Paul. 2008. "The Eyes of the Needles: A Sequential Model of Union Organizing Drives, 1999–2004." *Industrial and Labor Relations Review* 62(1): 8.

Fine, Janice. 2006. *Worker Centers: Organizing Communities at the Edge of the Dream.* Ithaca, N.Y.: Cornell University Press.

Fisher-Hoch, Susan P., Anne R. Rentfro, Jennifer J. Salinas, Adriana Perez, H. Shelton Brown, Belinda M. Reininger, Blanca I. Restrepo, MD, J. Gaines Wilson, MD, Monir Hossain, Mohammad H. Rahbar, Craig M. Hanis, and Joseph B. McCormick. 2010. "Unexpectedly High Prevalence of Obesity and Diabetes and the Impact of Socioeconomic Status in a Minority Community: The Cameron County Hispanic Cohort." Unpublished paper, University of Texas at Brownsville.

Freeman, Richard. 2005a. "Labor Market Institutions Without Blinders: The Debate over Flexibility and Labor Market Performance." Working paper 11286. Cambridge, Mass.: National Bureau of Economic Research (April).

————. 2005b. "Fighting for Other Folks' Wages: The Logic and Illogic of Living Wage Campaigns." *Industrial Relations* 44(1): 14–31.

————. 2007. "Do Workers Want Unions? More Than Ever." Briefing paper 182. Washington, D.C.: Economic Policy Institute (February).

Fremstad, Shawn. 2008. "Measuring Poverty and Economic Inclusion." Washington, D.C.: Center for Economic Policy and Research (December). Available at: http://www.cepr.net/documents/publications/2008-12-Measuring-Poverty-and -Economic-Inclusion.pdf.

FutureWorks. 2004. "Building Essential Skills through Training (BEST): Final Evaluation Report." Boston: Commonwealth Corporation (September).

Gabel, Jon R., Heidi Whitmore, and Jeremy Pickreign. 2007. "Report from Massachusetts: Employers Largely Support Health Care Reform and Few Signs of Crowd-Out Appear." *Health Affairs* (Web Exclusives) 27(1): w19.

Gabel, Jon R., Heidi Whitmore, Jeremy Pickreign, Will Sellheim, ShovaKC, and Valerie Bassett. 2008. "After the Mandates: Massachusetts Employers Continue to Support Health Reform as More Firms Offer Coverage." *Health Affairs* (Web Exclusives) 27(6): w568.

Gardner, Marylyn. 2007. "When a Layoff Is the Reward for Experience." *Christian Science Monitor*, April 16, p. 13.

Gautié, Jérôme, and John Schmitt, eds. 2010. *Low-Wage Work in the Wealthy World.* New York: Russell Sage Foundation.

Gilmer, Robert W., Matthew Gurch, and Thomas Wang. 2001. "Texas Border Cities: An Income Growth Perspective." A report for the Federal Reserve Bank of Dallas, June.

Goldin, Claudia, and Lawrence Katz. 2008. *The Race Between Education and Technology.* Cambridge, Mass.: Harvard University Press.

Goldstein, Bruce, Marc Lander, Laurence Norton, and Catherine Ruckelshaus. 1999. "Enforcing Fair Labor Standards in the Modern American Sweatshop: Rediscovering the Statutory Definition of Employment." *UCLA Law Review* 46(April): 983.

Good Jobs First. 2009. "High Road or Low Road? Job Quality in the New Green Economy." *Good Jobs First* (February): 25.

Gopinath, Sumanth. 2005. "Community Organizing and Economic Development in the University-Hospital City." Mimeo. New Haven, Conn.: Yale University, Working Group on Globalization and Culture.

Gray, Garry, and Susan Silbey. 2010. "Inside the Organization: The Regulator as Ally, Threat, and Obstacle." Paper presented at Law and Society Annual Meetings, Chicago (May).

Greenhouse, Stephen. 2000. "Deliverymen to Get $3 Million to Settle Wage Case." *New York Times*, December 8.

Groshen, Erica. 1991. "Sources of Intra-Industry Wage Dispersion: How Much Do Employers Matter?" *Quarterly Journal of Economics* (August): 869–84.

Grote, Kurt D., Edward H. Levine, and Paul D. Mango. 2006. "U.S. Hospitals for the Twenty-First Century." *McKinsey Quarterly* (August). Available at: https://www.mckinseyquarterly.com/US_hospitals_for_the_21st_century_1824.

Handel, Michael. 2005. "Trends in Perceived Job Quality, 1989 to 1998." *Work and Occupations* 32(1): 66–94.

Hanushek, Eric, and Ludger Woessmann. 2008. "The Role of Cognitive Skills in Economic Development." *Journal of Economic Literature* 46(3): 607–68.

Harris, Seth. 2010. Statement before the Senate Committee on Health, Education, Labor, and Pensions, June 17.

Hausman, Jerry, and Ephraim Leibtag. 2007. "Consumer Benefits from Increased Competition in Shopping Outlets: Measuring the Effect of Wal-Mart." *Journal of Applied Econometrics* 22: 1157–77.

Hertz, Tom. 2006. "Understanding Mobility in America." Washington, D.C.: Center for American Progress (April 26).

Hilton, Margaret, ed. 2008. *Research on Future Skill Demands: A Workshop Summary.* Washington, D.C.: National Academy Press.

Hinkin, Timothy R., and J. Bruce Tracey. 2000. "The Cost of Turnover." *Cornell Hotel and Restaurant Administration Quarterly* 41(3): 14–22.

Holzer, Harry. 2004. "Encouraging Job Advancement Among Low-Wage Workers: A New Approach." Policy brief 30. Washington, D.C.: Brookings Institution (May).

Holzer, Harry, and Robert Lerman. 2009. "America's Forgotten Middle-Skill Jobs." Washington, D.C.: Workforce Alliance.

Holzer, Harry, Steven Raphael, and Michael Stoll. 2006. "Employers in the Boom: How Did the Hiring of Less-Skilled Workers Change During the 1990s?" *Review of Economics and Statistics* 88(2): 283–99.

Horwitt, Sanford D. 1992. *Let Them Call Me Rebel; Saul Alinsky: His Life and Legacy.* New York: Vintage Books.

Howes, Candace. 2005. "Living Wages and Retention of Homecare Workers in San Francisco." *Industrial Relations* 44(1): 139–63.

Hudson, Gerry, Joel Rogers, and Phil Thompson. 2008. "Eyes on the Prize: Program Architecture of Emerald Cities." Memo to "interested parties," December 31. Available at: http://www.efficiencycities.org/wp-content/uploads/resources/EyesOnThePrize.pdf.

Interagency Task Force on Employee Misclassification. 2008. "Report to Governor Jennifer Granholm." Lansing: Michigan Department of Labor and Economic Growth (July 1).

Interfaith Workers Justice. 2008. "Building Justice: Interfaith Workers Justice Report on Residential Construction and Pulte Homes." Chicago: Interfaith Workers Justice (May).

Jacobs, Elizabeth, and Jacob Hacker. 2008. "The Rising Instability of American Family Incomes, 1969–2004." Briefing paper 213. Washington, D.C.: Economic Policy Institute (May 28).

Jacoby, Sanford. 2004. *Employing Bureaucracy: Managers, Unions, and the Transformation of Work in the Twentieth Century.* Mahwah, N.J.: Lawrence Erlbaum. (Originally published in 1985 by Columbia University Press under the title *Employing Bureaucracy: Managers, Unions, and the Transformation of Work in American Industry, 1900–1945.*)

Jencks, Christopher, Lauri Perman, and Lee Rainwater. 1988. "What Is a Good Job? A New Measure of Labor-Market Success." *American Journal of Sociology* 93(6): 1322–57.

Kain, Thomas J., and Cecilia E. Rouse. 1995. "Labor Market Returns to Two- and Four-Year Colleges." *American Economic Review* 85(3): 600–614.

Kalleberg, Arne. 2011. *Good Jobs, Bad Jobs: The Rise of Polarized and Precarious Employment Systems in the United States, 1970s to the 2000s.* New York: Russell Sage Foundation.

Kazee, Nicole, Michael Lipsky, and Cathie Jo Martin. 2008. "Outside the Big Box." *Boston Review* (July/August).

King, Christopher T., Tara Carter Smith, and Daniel G. Schroeder. 2009. "Evaluating Local Workforce Investments: Results for Short- and Long-Term Training in Austin (TX)." Austin: University of Texas, LBJ School of Public Affairs, Ray Marshall Center for the Study of Human Resources. Presented to the thirty-first annual research conference of the Association for Public Policy Analysis and Management (APPAM), Washington, D.C. (November).

Kochan, Thomas A. 2009. "Expert Report: Evaluation of Wal-Mart's Performance Management, Incentive, and Control Systems and Their Relation to Unpaid Work of Hourly Associates." Unpublished paper, Massachusetts Institute of Technology, Sloan School of Management.

Kochan, Thomas, Adrienne Eaton, Robert McKersie, and Paul Adler. 2009. *Healing Together: The Labor Management Partnership at Kaiser Permanente.* Ithaca, N.Y.: Cornell University Press.

Kopczuk, Wojiech, Emmanuel Saez, and Jae Song. 2010. "Earnings Inequality and Mobility in the United States: Evidence from Social Security Data Since 1937." *Quarterly Journal of Economics* 125(1): 95.

Korshak, Stuart R. 2000. "A Labor-Management Partnership." *Cornell Hotel and Restaurant Administration Quarterly* 41(2): 14–29.

Koys, Daniel. 2001. "The Effects of Employee Satisfaction, Organizational Citizenship Behavior, and Turnover on Organizational Effectiveness." *Personnel Psychology* 54(1): 101–14.

Krueger, Alan, and Mikael Lindahl. 2001. "Education for Growth: Why and for Whom." *Journal of Economic Literature* 39(4): 1101–36.

Krueger, Alan, and Lawrence Summers. 1988. "Efficiency Wages and the Inter-Industry Wage Structure." *Econometrica* 56(2): 259–93.

Kutz, Gregory D. 2008. "Case Studies from Ongoing Work Show Examples in

Which Wage and Hour Division Did Not Adequately Pursue Labor Violations." Statement before the House Committee on Education and Labor, July 15. GAO-08-973T.

Lacey, T. Alan, and Benjamin Wright. 2009. "Occupational Employment Projections to 2018." *Monthly Labor Review* 132(11): 82–123.

Lang, Joel. 2006. "The Fight to Cure a Community's Ills." *Hartford Courant*, May 21.

Lasowski, Anne-Marie. 2008. "Fair Labor Standards Act: Better Use of Available Resources and Consistent Reporting Could Improve Compliance." Statement before the House Committee on Education and Labor, July 15. GAO-08-962T.

Lee, Eungkyoon. 2005. "Why Did They Comply While Others Did Not? Environmental Compliance of Small Firms and Implications for Regulation." Ph.D. diss., Massachusetts Institute of Technology, Department of Urban Studies and Planning (September).

Lemieux, Thomas. 2006. "Increasing Residual Wage Inequality: Compositional Effects, Noisy Data, or Rising Demand for Skill?" *American Economic Review* 96(3): 461–98.

Leonard, Herman, and Orson Watson. 2006. "Integrated Packaging Corporation: Struggling to Do the Right Thing." Case N9-306-111. Boston: Harvard Business School (September 11).

Lester, T. William. 2009. "The Impact of Living Wage Laws on Urban Economic Development Patterns and the Local Business Climate: Evidence from California Cities." Berkeley: University of California, Institute for Research on Labor and Employment.

Lester, T. William, and Ken Jacobs. 2010. "Creating Good Jobs in Our Communities: How Higher Wage Standards Affect Economic Development and Employment." Washington, D.C.: Center for American Progress (November).

Lichtenstein, Nelson. 2002. *State of the Union.* Princeton, N.J.: Princeton University Press.

Lipset, Seymour Martin, Martin Trow, and James Coleman. 1962. *Union Democracy.* New York: Anchor.

Lipsky, Michael. 1980. *Street-Level Bureaucracy: Dilemmas of the Individual in Public Service.* New York: Russell Sage Foundation.

Locke, Richard, Fei Qin, and Alberto Brause. 2007. "Does Monitoring Improve Labor Standards? Lessons from Nike." *Industrial and Labor Relations Review* 61(1): 3–31.

Lopreste, Pamela, Gregory Acs, Caroline Ratcliffe, and Katie Vinopal. 2009. "Who Are Low-Wage Workers?" Research brief. Washington: U.S. Department of Health and Human Services, Assistant Secretary for Planning and Evaluation (February).

Madland, David, and Michael Paarlberg. 2008. "Making Contracting Work for the United States: Government Spending Must Lead to Good Jobs." Washington, D.C.: Center for American Progress (December).

Maguire, Sheila, Joshua Freely, Carol Clymer, Maureen Conway, and Deena Schwartz. 2010. "Tuning In to Local Labor Markets: Findings from the Sectoral Employment Study." Report. *Public/Private Ventures* (July).

Marcotte, Dave E., Thomas Bailey, Carey Borkoski, and Greg S. Kienzl. 2005. "The Returns of a Community College Education: Evidence from the National Education Longitudinal Survey." *Educational Evaluation and Policy Analysis* 27(summer): 157–75.

Mayfield, Marcia. 2010. "The Business of Caring: Ararat Nursing Facility." Washington, D.C., and New York: Paraprofessional Health Care Institute and Hitachi Foundation.

McKinsey Global Institute. 2001. "U.S. Productivity Growth, 1995–2000." Washington, D.C.: McKinsey Global Institute (October).

Mikelson, Kelley, and Demetra Nightingale. 2004. "Estimating Public and Private Expenditures on Occupational Training in the United States." Report prepared for the U.S. Department of Labor, Employment, and Training Administration. Washington, D.C.: The Urban Institute.

Mishel, Lawrence. 2010. "Top Group Takes Large Slice of Income Growth." Washington, D.C.: Economic Policy Institute (September 8). Available at: http://www.epi.org/economic_snapshots/entry/top_incomes_grow_while_bottom_incomes_stagnate/.

Moffitt, Robert, and Peter Gottschalk. 2008. "Trends in the Transitory Variances of Male Earnings in the U.S., 1970–2004." Working paper. Boston: Boston College (December).

Moynihan, Daniel. 1969. *Maximum Feasible Misunderstanding: Community Action in the War on Poverty.* New York: Free Press.

Nelson, Richard, and Sidney Winter. 1982. *An Evolutionary Theory of Economic Change.* Cambridge, Mass.: Harvard University Press.

Neumark, David, and Scott Adams. 2000. "Do Living Wage Ordinances Reduce Urban Poverty?" Working paper 7606. Cambridge, Mass.: National Bureau of Economic Research (March).

Neumark, David, Brandon Wall, and Junfu Zhang. 2011. "Do Small Businesses Create More Jobs? New Evidence for the United States from the National Establishment Time Series." *Review of Economics and Statistics* 93(1): 16–29.

Neumark, David, Junfu Zhang, and Stephen Ciccarella. 2005. "The Effects of Wal-Mart on Local Labor Markets." Working paper 11982. Cambridge, Mass.: National Bureau of Economic Research (November).

Newman, Katherine. 1999. *Falling from Grace: Downward Mobility in the Age of Affluence.* Berkeley: University of California Press.

Oreopolous, Philip, Marianne Page, and Ann Huff Stevens. 2008. "The Intergenerational Effects of Worker Displacement," *Journal of Labor Economics* 26(July): 455–83.

Organisation for Economic Co-operation and Development (OECD). Various years. *Employment Outlook.* Paris: OECD.

Osterman, Paul. 1999. *Securing Prosperity: How the American Labor Market Has Changed and What to Do About It.* Princeton, N.J.: Princeton University Press.

———. 2002. *Gathering Power: The Future of Progressive Politics in America.* Boston: Beacon Press.

———. 2007. *Gathering Power: The Future of Progressive Politics in America.* Boston: Beacon Press.

Osterman, Paul, and Brenda Lautsch. 1996. "Project QUEST: A Report to the Ford Foundation." Cambridge, Mass.: Massachusetts Institute of Technology, Sloan School of Management (January).

———. 1998. "Changing the Constraints: A Successful Employment and Training Strategy." In *Jobs and Economic Development*, edited by Robert Giloth. Thousand Oaks, Calif.: Sage Publications.

Ottaviano, Gianmarco I. P., and Giovanni Peri. 2006. "Rethinking the Effects of Immigration on Wages." Working paper 12497. Cambridge, Mass.: National Bureau of Economic Research (August).

Pager, Devah, Bruce Western, and Bart Bonikowski. 2009. "Discrimination in a Low-Wage Labor Market: A Field Experiment." *American Sociological Review* 75(5): 777–99.

Passel, Jeffrey, and D'Vera Cohen. 2009. "A Portrait of Unauthorized Immigrants in the United States." Washington, D.C.: Pew Hispanic Center (April 14).

Perez-Pena, Richard. 2000. "Spitzer to Sue Supermarket over Wages of Deliverymen." *New York Times*, January 13.

Pew Research Center. 2010. "Favorable Ratings of Unions Fall Sharply." February 23. Available at: http://people-press.org/2010/02/23/favorability-ratings-of-labor-unions-fall-sharply/.

———. 2011. *Political Typology Survey, Feb, 2011.* Available at: http://people-press.org/question-search/?qid=1785173&PID=51&ccid=51#top (accessed May 19, 2011).

Pindus, Nancy M., Carolyn O'Brien, Maureen Conway, Conaway Haskins, and Ida Rademacher. 2004. "Evaluation of the Sectoral Employment Demonstration Program." Washington, D.C.: Urban Institute (June).

Piore, Michael J., and Andrew Schrank. 2006. "Trading Up: An Embryonic Model for Easing the Human Costs of Free Markets." *Boston Review* (September/October).

Piven, Francis Fox, and Richard Cloward. 1977. *Poor People's Movements: Why They Succeed and How They Fail.* New York: Pantheon Books.

Planmatics, Inc. 2000. "Independent Contractors: Prevalence and Implications for Unemployment Insurance Programs." Report. Rockville, Md.: U.S. Department of Labor (February).

Public Religion Research Institute. 2010. "American Values Survey: Nationwide Survey Solicits the Public's Views on Raising the Minimum Wage, September 1–14, 2010." Available at: http://www.spotlightonpoverty.org/workers_and_poverty_polling.aspx?id=6d5b51d3-125e-48fc-8090-198061f9d4d4.

Rademacher, Ida, Marshall Bear, and Maureen Conway. 2001. "Project QUEST: A Case Study of a Sectoral Employment Development Approach." Washington, D.C.: Aspen Institute (August).

Reddy, Sudeep. 2011. "Downturn's Ugly Trademark: Steep, Lasting Drop in Wages." *Wall Street Journal*, January 11: 1.

Reich, Michael, Peter Hall, and Ken Jacobs. 2005. "Living Wage Policies at the San Francisco Airport." *Industrial Relations* 44(1): 111.

Ruckelshaus, Catherine. 2008. "Labor's Wage War." *Fordham Urban Law Journal* 35(373): 389.

———. 2009. "NELP Summary of Independent Contractor Reforms: New State Activity." New York: National Employment Law Project (July).

Ruckelshaus, Catherine, and Bruce Goldstein. 2002. "From Orchards to the Internet: Confronting Contingent Worker Abuse." New York: National Employment Law Project.

Sabel, Charles, Dara O'Rourke, and Archon Fung. 2000. "Ratcheting Labor Standards: Regulation for Continuous Improvement in the Global Workplace." New York: Columbia University Law School (February).

Sandel, Michael. 1996. *Democracy's Discontent: America in Search of a Public Philosophy.* Cambridge, Mass.: Harvard University Press.

Sawhill, Isabel, and John Morton. 2007. *Economic Mobility: Is the American Dream Alive and Well?* Washington, D.C.: Economic Mobility Project (February 21).

Schmitt, John, and Ben Zipperer. 2009. "Dropping the Ax: Illegal Firings During Union Election Campaigns, 1951–2007." Washington, D.C.: Center for Economic and Policy Research (March).

Scott, Richard W. 1998. *Organizations: Rational, Natural, and Open Systems.* Saddle Brook, N.J.: Prentice-Hall.

Seavey, Dorie. 2004. "The Cost of Frontline Turnover in Long-Term Care." Better Jobs, Better Care (October). Available at: http://www.directcareclearinghouse.org/download/TOCostReport.pdf.

Simmons, Louise, and Stephanie Luce. 2009. "Community Benefits Agreements: Lessons from New Haven." *Working USA: The Journal of Labor and Society* 12: 97–111, 101.

Skocpol, Theda. 1996. *Clinton's Health Security Effort and the Turn Against Government in U.S. Politics.* New York: W. W. Norton.

Sonn, Paul K., and Tsedeye Gebreselassie. 2009. "The Road to Responsible Contracting: Lessons from States and Cities for Ensuring That Federal Contracting Delivers Good Jobs and Quality Services." New York: National Employment Law Project (June).

Stevens, Ann Huff, and Jessamyn Schaller. 2009. "Short-Run Effects of Parental Job Loss on Children's Academic Achievement." Working paper 15480. Cambridge, Mass.: National Bureau of Economic Research (November).

Streeck, Wolfgang. 1997. "Beneficial Constraints: On the Economic Limits of Rational Voluntarism." In *Contemporary Capitalism: The Embeddedness of Institutions,* edited by J. Rodgers Hollingsworth and Robert Boyer. Cambridge: Cambridge University Press.

Sullivan, Daniel, and Till von Wachter. 2009. "Job Displacement and Mortality: An Analysis Using Administrative Data." *Quarterly Journal of Economics* 124(August): 1265–306.

Tavernise, Sabrina. 2011. "Ohio Town Sees Public Job as Only Route to Middle Class." *New York Times*, March 15: A19.

Theodore, Nik. 2010. "Realigning Labor: Toward a Framework for Collaboration Between Labor Unions and Day Labor Worker Centers." Washington, D.C.: Neighborhood Funders Group.

Theodos, Brett, and Robert Bednarzik. 2006. "Earnings Mobility and Low-Wage Workers in the United States." *Monthly Labor Review* (July): 34–47.

Thernstrom, Stephan. 1964. *The Other Bostonians: Poverty and Progress in the American Metropolis, 1880–1970.* Cambridge, Mass.: Harvard University Press.

Thomas, Sarah. 2010. "Cafeteria Workers Fight for Jobs." *Boston Globe*, April 4.

Thompson, Jeff, and Jeff Chapman. 2006. "The Economic Impact of Local Living Wages." Briefing paper 170. Washington, D.C.: Economic Policy Institute (February 16).

Urban Institute. 2006. "Five Questions for Signe-Mary McKernan and Caroline Ratcliffe." August 23. Available at: http://www.urban.org/toolkit/fivequestions/Mckernan_Ratcliffe.cfm.

U.S. Bureau of the Census. Various years. *Current Population Survey.* Washington: U.S. Bureau of the Census.

Vogel, David. 1995. *Trading Up: Consumer and Environmental Regulation in a Global Economy.* Cambridge, Mass.: Harvard University Press.

Von Wachter, Till. 2011. "Jobs Deficit and Job Growth: Unemployment and the Consequences for Workers." Champaign, Ill.: Employment Policy Research Network (January).

Waldinger, Roger D. 1998. "Helots No More: A Case Study of the Justice for Janitors Campaign in Los Angeles." In *Organizing to Win: New Research on Union Strategies*, edited by Kate Bronfenbrenner, Ronald Seeber, and Rudolf Oswald. Ithaca, N.Y.: ILR Press.

Waldron, Tom, Brandon Roberts, and Andrew Reamer. 2004. "Working Hard and Falling Short: America's Working Families and the Pursuit of Economic Security." A report for the Annie E. Casey Foundation, Baltimore, Md. (October).

Wall Street Journal. 2010. "Rival Chains Secretly Fund Opposition to Wal-Mart." *Wall Street Journal*, June 7.

Waltman, Jerold. 2000. *The Politics of the Minimum Wage.* Urbana: University of Illinois Press.

Warren, Mark R., and Richard L. Wood. 2001. "Faith-Based Organizing: The State of the Field." Report to the Interfaith Funders, Jericho, N.Y. Available at: http://comm-org.wisc.edu/papers2001/faith/faith.htm.

Weil, David. 2005. "Public Enforcement/Private Monitoring: Evaluating a New Approach to Regulating the Minimum Wage." *Industrial and Labor Relations Review* 58(2): 238–57.

———. 2009. "Rethinking the Regulation of Vulnerable Work in the U.S.: A Sector-Based Approach." *Journal of Industrial Relations* 51(3): 411–30.

———. 2010a. "Market Structure and Compliance: Why Janitorial Franchising Leads to Labor Standards Problems." Boston: Boston University (September 20).

———. 2010b. *Improving Workplace Conditions Through Strategic Enforcement: A Report to the Wage and Hour Division.* Boston: Boston University.

———. 2010c. "A Green Industrial Relations System for Construction: Challenges and Opportunities." Paper presented to the annual meeting of the Labor and Employment Relations Association (LERA), Atlanta (January 3–5, 2010). Paper revised January 30, 2010.

Weir, Margaret. 1992. *Politics and Jobs: The Boundaries of Employment Policy in America.* Princeton, N.J.: Princeton University Press.

Whiting, Basil. 2005. "The Retention and Advancement Demonstration Project (RAD): A 'Win-Win' for Manufacturers and Their Workers at Entry and Near-Entry-Levels." Washington, D.C.: National Association of Manufacturers, Center for Workforce Success, Manufacturing Institute (August).

Whitman, James. 2007. "Consumerism Versus Producerism: A Study of Comparative Law." *Yale Law Journal* 117(3): 340–406.

Wilkinson, Richard, and Kate Pickett. 2009. "Income Inequality and Social Dysfunction." *Annual Review of Sociology* 35: 493–511.

Wolf-Powers, Laura. 2010. "Community Benefits Agreements and Local Government: A Review of Recent Evidence." *Journal of the American Planning Association* 76(2): 142.

Womack, James, Daniel Jones, and Daniel Roos. 2007. *The Machine That Changed the World.* New York: Free Press.

Yu, Kyoung-Hee. 2008. "Between Bureaucracy and Social Movements: Careers in the Justice for Janitors." Ph.D. diss., Massachusetts Institute of Technology, Alfred P. Sloan School of Management (June).

Zuckerman, Ezra. 2004. "Structural Incoherence and Stock Market Activity." *American Sociological Review* 69(3): 405–32.

INDEX

Boldface numbers refer to figures and tables.